Lime Creek

O D Y S S E Y

STEVEN J MEYERS

Lime Creek

ODYSSEY

PHOTOGRAPHS BY THE AUTHOR

Fulcrum, Inc.
1989

Book Design by
Bryan Dahlberg

Printed in the United States
1 2 3 4 5 6 7 8 9 0

LIBRARY OF CONGRESS
CATALOGING-IN-PUBLICATION DATA

Meyers, Steven J.
Lime Creek Odyssey

1. Nature   2. Nature—Philosophy
I. Title

QB81.M584   1989   508'01'3   88-32705
ISBN 1-55591-037-8

Fulcrum, Inc.
Golden, Colorado

For K.B.

CONTENTS

INTRODUCTION

The contemporary mind seems to have reserved a rather distant and peculiar place for nature. Some (the least perceptive among us) feel that nature is simply the place where we find the resources to fuel our existence. Some feel compelled occasionally to travel to this place called nature in order to restore their mental health or to learn the lessons that nature has to teach. We are surrounded by magazines, books and documentary films that show us the incredible value, beauty, richness and diversity of a distant nature. In each case—as a thing to be exploited, a place to visit or a place from which to learn—nature exists as something separate from ourselves.

Humans have walked upon the earth for countless millennia, but for most of that time travel was limited. Magazines, books and films did not exist. Exposure to distant places and events did not occur. Each individual had access to his own observations and his own immediate place. Shared experience took the form of a cultural inheritance, embodied in slowly evolving rituals and oral tradition. These too were rooted in place. Even those who ranged through a relatively wide expanse of terrain—moving with the seasons, following good weather and migrating game—moved at a pace slow enough to

1

allow a constant sense of immediacy. *Nature*, I suspect, would have been a foreign concept in this context. Life absorbed it, and it could not be conceived of as a separate entity. I believe there are advantages to be had in regaining this perspective.

Contemporary literature reflects the values of the societies within which it flourishes. Much writing ranges widely, explores the distant, details the strange and revels in the obscure. The tendency is not strictly modern. We find evidence of it for as long as there has been literature. Homer expressed the Greek heroic ideal by sending Odysseus off to a distant war and then on a roundabout journey home. His travels to faraway lands were filled with discovery, and we are led to believe that such a life brings great knowledge. Appearing much less heroic and learned in these tales was Penelope, who waited at home for the return of her husband.

Contemporary ideals of heroism, greatness, and significant exploration seem to follow the Greek heroic model. Discoveries aren't discoveries at all unless they are made far from home in an exotic land. Yet when I think of Odysseus and Penelope, it is not the warrior-traveler who commands my respect and admiration. His heroism was often the result of circumstance and even more often the result of foolhardiness and bravado. He shows little evidence of profound knowledge or wisdom. Are we to believe that Penelope really did nothing for 20 years but weave or that she learned nothing while waiting for the return of the conquering hero? I think it more likely that her time was filled with an exploration of a vastly more significant place—her home—and that her thoughts, not occupied by repeated immediate threats to life and limb, were occupied with far richer responses than fleeing or fighting. Her journey, as yet unrecorded, was probably at least equal to that of her better-known husband, and the lessons we might learn from her odyssey are perhaps more significant.

"Lime Creek odyssey" might appear to be something of an

oxymoron. Like British cuisine and military intelligence, a Lime Creek odyssey seems to make little sense. The physical setting is too small. Within the perspective of an earlier time, however, the title makes a good deal of sense. An odyssey need not involve a long journey, simply a profound one. A place need not be exotic in order to serve as a springboard for discovery. In fact, I wonder if long journeys serve us as well as explorations of our own homes. Perhaps it is best to explore the meaning of place at our doorstep.

Lime Creek is both a place and an emblem. For me it is a distillation of the character of a region I know as home and within which I live. It is neither far away, nor separate from me. We live here, together.

The creek is not particularly long or broad. Its main stem travels roughly 12 miles from its headwaters (a few miles southwest of Silverton, deep in the heart of the San Juan Mountains of southwestern Colorado) to its terminus at the confluence with Cascade Creek. Its width ranges from a few feet at its beginnings to the 25-foot or so width of its widest shallow riffles. Yet of all the streams I have sat beside, walked along or waded through, I find it the most powerful in experience and memory.

It begins in the glacial cirques of high peaks and never leaves the mountains, but the terrain and climatic zones it travels through are quite varied. It can be a calm meander through a lush mountain meadow or a tumultuous roaring torrent through a narrow, rock-walled gorge. Its banks can be stark with the limited but beautiful life of the tundra, or they can be verdant with the complexity of a mountain forest nourished by rich moist soil. In short, Lime Creek is everything a mountain stream should be.

In the San Juans there are more remote streams that are just as varied and beautiful. There are less accessible streams that lend credence to the illusion that a personally discovered stream belongs to you and you alone. A highway follows the course of the Lime Creek valley and a dirt road meanders beside the stream where the deep gorges give way to gentler terrain. In an area so dominated by wilderness, it must seem strange that this relatively accessible creek should become an emblem of place.

The history of man in the San Juans is long and complex. Utes hunted here and lived among the peaks long before Europeans arrived. The Spanish came from the south and other Europeans came from the east during the period of preliminary exploration that ended rather abruptly with the Civil War. After the war, prospectors and miners, road builders and railroaders came to extract the gold and silver found in the rocky veins of the heavily mineralized mountains. They carried it away on the backs of mules, in horse-drawn wagons and railroad gondola cars. As towns were established, civilization soon followed.

To ignore the presence of man here would be naive, but there is wilderness here too—land that shows little evidence that man exists. The San Juans, like many other wild places, straddle the border between wilderness and human habitation. Lime Creek, wild yet well explored, is a manifestation of this truth. It is not my private stream, no matter how compelling the illusion may be. The creek helps me to remember that even apparently undiscovered, remote streams do not become mine alone upon discovery.

Beyond Lime Creek's varied terrain and habitat, beyond its existence as a wild yet known place, Lime Creek embraces all that the San Juans are for me because it is a place where I have spent a great deal of time. I have waded the streambed, walked the woods and climbed many of the peaks surrounding the valley. From here the creek leaves the mountains to join the ever-increasing flows that eventually become the Pacific Ocean. Here in the San Juans, however, it is a headwater, a source—a

Introduction

good place for the discovery of one's own roots and meaning.

It seems appropriate for me to wander this little valley while others, more heroic, journey to Nepal, the Arctic, the tropical rain forest. This personal odyssey of *place*, this exploration of a mountain stream, is also a journey in the discovery of self, and a search for an appropriate definition of man's place in the broader reality of nature. I stay at home, like Penelope, believing that one's home is the proper place for such an odyssey.

Of
Meatballs,
Swiss Cheese
and Sponges

1

Much of the time I spent with Lime Creek, especially when I first explored the drainage, was in the high ground above the valley floor. My early memories of the area are dominated by mountains. Two peaks, in particular, stand out, one because I have been on its summit so often, and the other, though I have climbed it only once, because that experience was quite special. The two mountains sit facing each other across the Lime Creek canyon, their flanks defining a gorge that has come to be one of my favorites in the Lime Creek drainage. The peak climbed often is Engineer Mountain. The peak climbed only once is North Twilight Peak. Together these two peaks frame Lime Creek through the middle of her course; they frame the course of my experience of the creek as well.

Engineer Mountain sits alone, unlike most others in the San Juans. Not part of a larger group of mountains, its ridges don't lead directly to other peaks. Its sphinxlike posture comes from this isolation and from its distinctive shape, which is unmistakable and easily identified. The mountain is long and narrow with a high, massive cone-shaped summit that is connected by a long spinelike ridge to a second, lower summit. From either of these summits or the ridge connecting them, the mountain falls away to the valley floor. Engineer sits between the summits of the West Needles (the mountain massif that includes North Twilight Peak) and the high mountain group that lies between the towns of Silverton and Rico. From the top of this relatively isolated peak, you can look out on a stunning panorama, including a broad green-floored and red sandstone-walled glacial valley that extends southward toward Durango. Most locals contemplate a trip to the summit, and many make the climb. Many times I have climbed this mountain with neighbors, with friends and with first-time visitors to the San Juan Mountains who want a look at the lay of the land.

A climb up Engineer is not particularly difficult in relation to the scale of difficulty used by experienced climbers, but it is quite difficult when viewed in terms of the scale of difficulty used by hikers. When approached by the usual, most beautiful route on the northeast ridge, it is a very difficult, exposed hike. A trip to the summit often involves a mixture of sloping meadows, deep woods, loose rock, rock chimneys and steep snow; yet, if attempted in the company of someone who knows the route, it is a climb that a hiker without any climbing experience but with a little courage and pluck can make. As a result, strange collections of people often group together to work their way up the ridge to the summit. Experienced climbers, who often seek more difficult ascents, will accompany hikers who have never been on a mountain before. All go for the same reason: the beauty of the mountain and the anticipated beauty of the climb.

I have had the good fortune to find time to go up Engineer nearly every year since the San Juans became my home just over a decade ago. Some years I have made the trip several times. Most often I have spent the day on the mountain in the company of non-climbers, and my most memorable experiences there are filled with the wide eyes and wider smiles of these companions. The mountain always fills me with wonder and profound pleasure; my companions often do too.

Several years ago I made the trip with two friends and a new acquaintance. We were an odd assortment. Two of us lived in the mountains; the other two were then living in the flatlands. We were a writer and a photographer, a therapist and a musician. Two of us had been up the mountain many times, often together; the other two not at all.

The two flatlanders, however, were not newcomers to wilderness. Both had, in their own way, dedicated a large part of their lives, talents and energies to the exploration and celebration of the natural world. Their trip to visit us in the San Juans was an extension of a journey they had just made to the desert and canyon country of southeastern Utah—a journey that included an attempt to write and perform music as a response to the moods of the canyons. Before they returned home, Nancy and David decided to visit the San Juans and to climb Engineer Mountain. Our journey up the mountain was a metaphorical complement to the canyons. The climb, like the river trip to the canyons, involved music in response to place. In our packs we carried our usual supplies: extra clothing, water, food and a rope just in case someone felt a need for a belay through one of the few tricky spots. In addition we carried some unusual gear: double ocarinas, a few simple percussion instruments and an oboe.

We began our climb in the marshy meadows at the top of Coal Bank Hill, working slowly up through the steep wet grasses and false hellebore. In midsummer, the false hellebore was nearly up to our chests. Local belief has it that the height of these plants indicates the depth of the coming winter's snows. If this was true, it was going to be a heavy snow year. At the crest of the grassy slope we entered a series of limestone benches, each several hundred yards wide, each heavily forested with spruce and balsam fir, the forest floor an alternating world of snow-melt bog and flower-covered meadow.

LIME CREEK ODYSSEY

Is there anything that simultaneously reconciles the seemingly irreconcilable opposites of flamboyance and subtlety as well as the alpine forest floor? Color more showy and brilliant than any I have seen anywhere else exists along with flowers so small and delicate, so carefully hidden in the interstices, that they, but for direct attention and active seeking, remain hidden from view. This apparent contradiction exists in all of the natural world, but its manifestation in the alpine forest is no less startling for this realization.

As we continued our hike, forested benches and limestone cliffs filled with the fossilized remains of millions of tiny creatures gradually gave way to a rolling grassy slope, above which was treeline and then the massive rocky cone that is the peak.

Our climb took us through shattered rock along a ridge formed initially by glaciation and later by the continuous melt-freeze fracturing that is typical in the volcanic and sedimentary formations of the San Juans. Climbers used to the solid granite, hard cracks and vertical faces of places like Yosemite find the San Juans nerve-racking. Even modest slopes can be dangerous because of the loose rock. Without a basic sense of trust in the relative stability of broken rock in repose and the ability to quickly abandon a platform that proves to be unreliable, even a relatively easy climb, such as the one up Engineer, can become a fearful experience. With little relief the climb crosses scree, talus and precariously balanced boulders, but the ridge emerges from all of this, an obvious and safe path as it winds its way to the summit.

Along the way, each change in the rock signals a new rhythm to the climb. The steep tundra of the base gives way to a band of relatively stable red sedimentary rock. The red rock becomes a fractured band of white rock that slides with little provocation. The white rock becomes another band of red, then a band of tan rock that is more stable but much steeper. Climbing out of the last chimney in the tan band, the large,

12

balanced blocks of gray conglomerate on the summit ridge come into view.

At the bottom we had climbed steep slopes with long confident strides, then changed to short tentative steps in the loose scree. From here the rock had gradually steepened until nearly vertical, and we resorted to stair-stepping, climbing motions with our hands and feet. At last we had emerged on the summit ridge, where we moved once again with long, confident strides toward the summit.

The view, as expected, was wonderful and so much more pleasant and rewarding for having been earned. I have flown through the San Juans quite a bit, sometimes in light aircraft, sometimes in large commercial jets, a few times in helicopters. The views during those flights, I must admit, were spectacular. I would whisk over and through drainages that I had spent days hiking and those that I wished I would someday hike. As jagged pinnacles of rock, high crags and steeply dropping ridges passed close below, with my feet planted on nothing but air, I saw more rugged land at one time than I once thought existed. But all that pales beside the experience of looking down from a mountain you have climbed. To be breathing hard with sweat glistening on your body, grinning as the view emerges at the summit, is an experience that can never be equaled in photographs or plane rides. The view that day with my three companions, though I had seen it many times before, was no exception.

The deep valley of the Animas River lay to the south beneath us, its waters and those of the valley's small lakes shining in the midday sun. To the north the high snow-covered peaks of the San Juans near Silverton reflected a light that appeared amplified, more than just a reflection of the sun's brilliance. To the west were the mountains and forested flats of the Hermosa Plateau. To the east rose the steep, massive face of North Twilight Peak and the pinnacles of the Needles Mountains behind it. Beneath our feet, Engineer's walls abruptly fell away to the valley floor, green and lush before us to the south, white and wintry behind us to the north. Can anyone be in such a place and not be deeply moved?

When I was a student I heard many discussions in literature and writing classes about romanticism, about the limits of language and about the need for writers to restrain emotion, to rein it in so that description and expression of personal passion avoid hyperbole, or worse, maudlin sentimentality. I was distressed to hear this once again in graduate school in reference to the visual media. Even more distressing was the stunning silence, in the upper levels of academia, in graduate seminars and colloquia, of the issue not being discussed at all. For the academically trained, the issue had been settled. Personal passion, love, beauty, agony, ecstasy, none of these were allowed to exist. We would be well advised, it seems, not to make ourselves appear stupid by bringing these themes out of the grave where they had been laid to rest. This is true for love stories, autobiographies, news reporting, novels, short stories, essays and poetry (God, yes, poetry), and, especially, it would seem, nature writing. Pure description when penned with skill is sufficient to evoke emotion. There is no need to overdo it.

Yet, what is someone to do with a memory like this? When we got to the summit, we smiled, laughed, sighed, sobbed and ate. We organized thoughts and packs. After we had each found a comfortable seat the instruments were distributed. We began to play, to make music. Those of us with little talent did what we could in support of those in whose hands and lips instruments became extensions of thought, of being. Music began to flow from our happiness into the air, and from the air into the world around us. And from the world around us, into us and back out again. Butterflies that had been fluttering nearby came closer and fluttered near our faces. A hawk that had been circling overhead came in low and slowly passed—

passed so close, in fact, that the wind moving through its wings made a sound we all heard above and in complement to our music. One by one we put down our double ocarinas, our wood blocks and sticks, and waited for Nancy to pick up her oboe. She did. A few tentative notes came out, notes that seemed to be searching for an anchor in the soil of the valley and a lift from the blue sky overhead. More notes came. Finally, a song. A song that flowed from the oboe as if the earth itself had written it. The light changed. A brightness of an intensity never seen down in the valley grew to envelop the mountaintop. Distinctions between rock and sound, light and rhythm ceased to exist. I cannot recall ever having heard a song so beautiful or so appropriate. That it was improvised, that it will never be heard again, that it belonged to that place and time made the memory more precious.

Is my description of this experience hyperbole? This telling isn't the half of it. Romantic? I guess so. Maudlin? I don't know. Sometimes life is more important than art (whatever art is) and truth more valuable than restraint. I'm a firm believer in passion and stupidity and life. I think these experiences are not ours to hoard; rather, they are ours to share. To pretend that the experience was less or other than what it was is not sophistication. It is pretentiousness in the extreme. Compared with a mountain some hundred-million years old, we're all a bit stupid and naive and unsophisticated. Coming down from the mountain, as we reluctantly did, doesn't mean abandoning the joy and wonder we shared there, no matter how strange it might have seemed when we got back to town. Part of holding the experience of a climb is being able to realize that it all really happened.

Many people eye North Twilight Peak, thinking someday they might like to climb one of the ridges or snow-filled gullies that lead to its apex. Many, I suspect, wonder what it would be like to sit on top and see what the surrounding mountains look

15

like from that vantage point. The desire is partially rooted in the knowledge that North Twilight Peak, unlike Engineer Mountain, sits in close proximity to the incredibly jagged and steep summits of the Needles Mountains and the Grenadier Range of the Weminuche Wilderness to the east. Few, however, make the climb.

The reasons are numerous. Any easy route up Twilight, any route that might be taken by an inexperienced hiker or climber, involves a fairly long slog through difficult country. Any direct ascent involves some rock climbing skill if the path follows one of the steep ridges or snow and ice climbing skill if it's a gully route. Still, vastly more difficult peaks are climbed in the San Juans, some frequently. North Twilight Peak is protected from the hordes of hikers because it's more than a hike, from the bulk of climbers because it's not one of the better-known climbs, and from both, I suspect, because it has escaped the rather dubious distinction of becoming a well-known destination, even though it has achieved some distinction as a scenic wonder when viewed from afar. North Twilight Peak is not a particularly high peak. Many who climb mountains seek vertical; a 13,000-foot summit is not as attractive as a 14,000-foot summit. While the logic of this attitude escapes me, I don't mind. It leaves some very nice country relatively untrammeled.

Strange wishes are known to develop and linger in the hearts of residents in this mountain-filled world, and I suspect the content of those wishes in some way sketches the outline of our response to the surroundings. A desire that began very soon after my arrival here, and grew until it became something of an obsession, was the wish to climb every peak that I could see from my home. The desire then grew to include all the peaks I see often. Nothing, as you might imagine, would be worse than having a wish whose limits are so obscure that they make fulfillment impossible. This was precisely the nature of this particular desire. I believe the technical term for this condition is *neurosis*; the common term, *no-win situation*. Climbing the peaks visible from home was relatively easy and very rewarding until I moved a few blocks and could see a few more peaks. The desire to climb all those, however, was never very realistic. My weekly 50-mile trip south to Durango for groceries, to see a movie, to buy a book reveals scores—no, hundreds—of peaks. A 26-mile trip north to the Ouray Hot Springs reveals hundreds more. And what of the summits that emerge when one of these peaks is finally climbed, summits that are seen repeatedly, with different aspects and personalities, as a person climbs more and more?

It didn't take me long to realize that a desire like the one to climb every peak often seen would soon lead me to madness, if indeed I had not already arrived. Being a practical person, I found my wish slowly transformed into one even more diffuse, even less definable, but one less likely to cause insanity. This wish was to climb peaks I see from home or peaks seen often that for some reason I find particularly attractive, either by virtue of their beauty, their mystery or their ability to make me think of them at the oddest moments and say, "Someday I've got to climb that thing." This desire was infinitely more manageable and infinitely more pleasant. In a very natural way it guided my choices about where I would go and what I would do for quite a while.

North Twilight Peak, or simply Twilight, as it is known by locals, was one of the peaks on that wish list. I saw it from the highway every time I went to town for groceries. I saw it across Lime Creek from the summit of Engineer Mountain every time I made a trip there. Often I would see its snow-covered flanks bathed in the pink glow of twilight when I returned from winter ski trips. Its steep snow-filled gullies and ridges rose up before me when I was hiking or fishing in the creek bottom. It is a strikingly beautiful mountain.

There was only one problem. A pleasing ascent by a good

route would require a degree of skill I did not possess when the idea of climbing Twilight first came to me. When learning to climb I found myself woefully inadequate on steep ice and snow. I discovered this when I attempted in ignorance an extremely difficult route up the north face of Mount Sneffels, about 30 miles north of Twilight, a route I thought might make a good warm-up climb for one of the snow-filled gullies I particularly liked on Twilight's north face. I escaped from Sneffels with my life and some very precious lessons in humility, but my confidence had been damaged severely in the process. After that escape, Twilight, for all my desire to climb its north face, looked to me more like K2 in the Karakoram than it had any right to do. Still, wishes being what they are, with something about falling off a horse dimly echoing in the deep recesses of consciousness, I set out to climb North Twilight Peak by the direct route up a steep snow gully on its north face. With me was a friend in whom I had great confidence as a snow climber and another friend with whom I had escaped physical damage if not ego-deflation on Sneffels.

While nearly everyone we knew who climbed at all could talk very authoritatively about the mountain (mountaineers, I was to learn much later, are very much like fishermen), they all responded when pressed, "Well, no, I've never actually climbed it." This great reservoir of experience and profound knowledge of the mountain among the climbing fraternity did little to soothe my fears. On the hike in—five miles of rolling limestone benches with alternating meadows and woods on a trail above Lime Creek—I stared at Twilight's face with the intensity of a convicted man gazing into the eyes of a towering judge who would soon pronounce sentence. My share of our bright and cheerful conversation was, I sadly admit, a sham. I was whistling in the dark.

In camp that night, my companions stayed up arguing about the names of the stars in the night sky. One lay flat on his back with a star guide in his hands and a headlamp on his head so he could see the star guide in the black of night. As I lay in my tent fighting fear and praying for sleep or death, anything that would end the interminable night, he repeatedly yelled to me, "Which way is North?" "What time is it?" "Well, damn, then that has to be Arcturus!" My other companion, calmly sitting on a log, repeated over and over, "I've been looking at the summer sky all my life. That is Vega." He with the headlamp then gave a discourse about the constellation Bootes and recited the story of the origin of wine from *Bulfinch's Mythology*. This useful reference was dutifully packed in along with headlamp, batteries, star chart, astronomy books, wildlife and flower identification guides, rope and ice axe, bivy tent, sleeping bag with pad, extra clothing, stove, food, and water. And, although he denies it to this day, I could swear I saw the hulking outline of a *Webster's Unabridged Dictionary* in the dark recesses of his pack. The argument ended shortly after midnight when Vega calmly rose through the trees to the high mountain skyline and took its rightful place in the summer sky. She on the log, admitting defeat, softly said, "I believe that's Vega rising now." He with the headlamp concurred. Mercifully, sleep then took me.

We rose from our bivouacs at dawn and began to heat water for tea and oatmeal. After a quick breakfast, we shouldered our packs and walked around Crater Lake to the alluvial fan that formed the bottom of the chute we would climb. Log Sitter and I, by virtue of our greater experience with ice axe and snow, tied into the ends of the rope. Headlamp tied into the middle. Log Sitter probably should have led the whole climb; she was certainly the best climber. I now believe that she sensed my apprehension and had greater faith in me than I had in myself. She wanted me to rediscover the joy and rhythm of climbing and to lose some of the fear. Her plan was for us to exchange the lead, each climbing above Headlamp, who would remain in the middle maintaining a belay. This would require no time-consuming retying, which would have been necessary if the three of us had exchanged leads on the climb. It would also place Headlamp in a position where he would receive a constant shower of cold, wet snow and ice chips as the leader, directly above him, cut-steps and handholds. He would thereby receive his due payment for having been proven correct by the midnight rising of Vega. It was a good plan.

We began slowly and quietly, exchanging the lead with every rope length. Gradually the lake below us fell away; we watched it between our feet as it became smaller and smaller. We climbed in the cool shade of high altitude and in good firm snow. When we reached the top a few hours later, the sun hit our faces for the first time. It dawned on me as suddenly as the unexpected warmth of the sun on my skin that I had been so busy moving, chopping and feeling the texture of the snow that I had never once thought to be afraid. A few weeks earlier, on Sneffels, I had learned not to underestimate a mountain or to overestimate my own ability. On Twilight I learned an equally valid corollary. The complete axiom ought to read: "Nothing is as easy it looks, nor as difficult." The rule, I have found, applies to a great deal more than climbing mountains.

Between Engineer Mountain and Twilight lies Lime Creek. I don't know how long it was before I came to see that valley as a volume and not a void, the space between the summits as a reality every bit as massive as the mountains themselves. Visual artists, dancers and architects speak of positive and negative space, of implied mass. We are all familiar with the classic reversing illusions. These drawings appear to be one thing, then become another, then switch back again. Whatever we see in the illusion, we have but one drawing. The drawing is not changing, our perception of it is. When we look at a drainage we may see either valleys or mountains, or perhaps each in turn. Neither, however, even an alternating perception, accurately sees the place.

There has been an ongoing discussion in cosmology that uses what I think are intriguing metaphors, although as a layman I am certain most of the ramifications escape me. I should think these metaphors would appeal to anyone drawn to the idea of mountains and drainages, positive and negative space, implied mass and the overriding issue of integrative vision.

Some scientists have found it useful to think of the cosmos as a collection of meatballs. That is, there is evidence to support the idea that the vast majority of space is an empty arena with occasional clumps of matter, occasional areas of mass density. Meatballs. Other scientists have found evidence for the belief that matter is the defining constant in the universe, that matter is the stuff of which the universe is made and therefore the areas without any mass density would be better represented as holes in a background of mass. Swiss cheese. These seemingly trivial metaphors have a great deal of organizing power, and each asserts a frame of reference capable of structuring research, the design of instruments and the inferences drawn from gathered data. Each is a compelling metaphor, yet neither, it seems, is quite adequate. Any reconciliation between these two models would require an overriding metaphor for the structure of the universe that could contain them both. What, do you suppose, would have the power to suck up the evidence for both meatballs and swiss cheese? How about a sponge!

A sponge is a fabric in which neither holes nor clumps dominate. It is a matrix of density and emptiness that, as metaphor, readily accounts for the cosmological phenomena of meatballs and swiss cheese. When seen as a model for the structure of the universe, it is not merely a physical object, but an idea through which experience may be ordered. The sponge, as metaphor, is not analytical; it is synthetic; it is integrative.

LIME CREEK ODYSSEY

This metaphor goes a long way toward resolving one of the fundamental conflicts of cosmology.

I think that if we are to understand something as rich and complex as a mountain drainage, we must begin to see mountains and valleys not as meatballs and swiss cheese—we must find a metaphor that unifies the tremendous diversity that is this place. Lime Creek exists in part because of the mountains that abide there, and in part because of the valleys that form the drainages. It is each of them and it is both of them. But it is more. Our experience of Lime Creek embraces its mountains and valleys. It embraces the creatures that dwell there, the plants that grow. It embraces the changes that take place with the passage of time. Most significantly, our experience of this complex and wonderful place embraces the fact of our existence as perceiving and feeling beings. Lime Creek is not simply a place of rock and soil, of air and water, of plants and animals. For us it is a place of the mind and heart as well.

Lime Creek lies between the pinnacle of my joys, my aspirations, my vision and the pinnacle of my fears, my doubts, my blindness. It is them and it is not. I feel good walking the streambed and more at home when knee-deep in those boisterous waters than anywhere I have yet been. This is part of the meaning of *place*. This is a step toward a new metaphor. This, I believe, is the nature of our odyssey.

A
Gothic
Romance

2
_____

W hy is it when we refer to the outdoors we so often say "the woods"? It struck me once as I was speaking with a friend about my intention to get outside, away from the confinement of my darkroom, that I almost always say "the woods" when I wish to refer to a wild place, whether the place I have in mind has trees or not. I tell people that I need to spend time alone "in the woods" even as I think of a tent pitched by a high alpine lake above treeline. I say "I need to get to the woods" when I want to escape for a while from town, even if I end up in the desert where the scattered piñon and juniper can hardly be construed as a forest. Of course, I also say "I'm going to the woods" when I am, indeed, heading for a forest trail or tree-shrouded trout stream.

The woods. This pair of words is magical for me, and I suspect for others. I'm not really sure I know why. As magical as the phrase, how much more magical to actually be in the forest.

The woods surrounding Lime Creek vary somewhat with elevation and aspect. In the upper reaches of the creek nothing exists that could be called a forest. Surrounding the creek are low shrubs and tundra. In sheltered stretches, warmed by south-facing slopes, willows crowd the banks and obscure the water from view. Some Engelmann spruce grow, their shape distorted by the harsh conditions of wind, radiation and extreme temperatures. Bristlecone pine (planted in various places to reclaim the drainage after the massive Lime Creek Burn of the late 19th century) struggle for growth here as well, but the feeling is one of openness and exposure rather than of nurturing forest.

A little farther down the tundra becomes populated, sparsely at first and then with increasing density, by the inhabitants of the spruce and fir belt. Larger, better-shaped Engelmann spruce and alpine fir combine to form a band of forest that blends naturally and gradually with the fir and aspen belt that it encounters lower still. In these two regions the forest becomes real forest, the woods we imagine when we contemplate sunlight filtering through high branches to fall softly on the forest floor, the woods we picture when we imagine the dappled golden light of autumn or rolling walks along cool, shaded trails. At its lowest elevations Lime Creek comes close to the trees, shrubs and flowers of the pine and oak forest that emerges a few miles downstream from its confluence with Cascade Creek, along the banks of the Animas River where ponderosa pine and gambel oak begin to appear, where alder begin to replace willows at streamside.

I often walk through a large, flat meadow of aspen roughly midway along the course of Lime Creek. The trees are mature and tall, their lower branches having long since withered, died and fallen. The burden of photosynthesis is now carried by leaves well above the forest floor. The slender white trunks of the trees rise from this floor, radiant and luminous. Although the forest is dense, there is no sense of confinement or darkness; the distinct impression is of open, glowing space. The lines of the trunks soar upward where they join the curving branches of the forest crown, a lofty region where individual trees lose identity in the vaulted ceiling of the forest roof. Light is diffused by the leaves and, against this subdued background, finds itself apparently magnified in those places where it passes unimpeded through openings in the canopy, brilliant rays striking the heights and sometimes descending to the very roots of the forest.

This aspen wood is a place that lifts the spirit in much the way intended by the builders of Gothic cathedrals. It is the sort of place often said to resemble them. In tourist areas (particularly those famous for their trees—the redwoods of California, the tall Douglas fir of the Northwest) it is not surprising that such places often have a name like *Cathedral Grove*. The similarity between the forest and the Gothic style is striking. What is odd, or appears so to me at least, is that we have no cathedrals with names like *Forest Light* or *Aspen Glade*.

Our culture, with its principally European roots, seems to have a problem with orientation, with the proper arranging of events in time and according to relative importance. Nowhere is this as true as in the matter of approaching and explaining nature. Oddly, when we attempt to articulate our feelings in the face of nature we forget which came first: natural experience or the products of civilization. Often in our experiences of nature and in our attempts to derive meaning from them we have a strong and unfortunate tendency to put the cart before the horse.

Oscar Wilde proposed that nature is a rather poor reflection of art. This attitude (once described by an aesthetician as much like saying that Andrew Carnegie was named after all those libraries) absurd as it seems, lies, if somewhat obscurely, at the root of many judgments and perceptions. Seeing the Gothic cathedral in the forest, rather than the other way around, would seem to be an error of this type.

The essence of the Gothic style cannot be readily isolated. Is it the sense of height or the seeming simplicity that results in this height (easily recognized when the Gothic cathedral is compared with the relatively clumsy bulk of the often equally lofty Romanesque cathedral)? Is it the quality and source of the light that suffuses the interior space or the shape and feel of the space itself? Is it found in the structural advances that made the delicacy and grace of Gothic vaulting possible or the affectations, not structurally necessary, that were often added to maintain elegance and symmetry? Is it found in the theology that dominated the thoughts of the reputed author of the Gothic style, Abbot Suger of 12th-century France? Or are his theology and vision rooted in something more basic, more ancient than the then-popular theories of the fifth-century Greek theologian Dionysius the Areopagite, whose ideas of mathematical proportion are said to have influenced the abbot as he built what is considered the first expression of the Gothic sentiment, the Abbey Church of Saint Denis?

It cannot be denied that there is a distinctive difference between the Gothic and that which preceded, but to what vision, to what combination of structure and intention, form and idea does the style owe its soul? I would argue that the inspiration for the Gothic cathedral came from a shared primal experience of the forest. I would further argue that to experience the forest as an expression of the Gothic style is very much like thinking that Carnegie was named after all those libraries.

Light filters through the high branches of the aspen wood much like the light of the clerestory. White aspen trunks soar upward into the heights of the forest crown much like the responds that carry the weight-bearing ribbing of the vaults to the floor of the cathedral. The forest glows. The forest soars. The forest was before the cathedral and will most likely remain long after the cathedral has gone. The Gothic cathedral is a magnificent expression of the forest and of our theological abstractions, an elegant distillation, a wondrous thing, but it is not the forest itself. Nor is it as rich.

The beauty of the forest, the experience of the forest, is so complex, so involved with the innumerable relationships among the components of the forest—with each other and with our-selves—that it would be impossible to identify the source of that beauty except to say that it lies in a perception of the whole. Threats to that beauty are also complex, but in Lime Creek there is one overriding threat that looms above all others. That is the loss of the pure sky and the unique light that make a walk in these woods so special. Unfortunately, the future of the skies above Lime Creek is not as clear as the limpid light that resides there now.

Lime Creek defines a valley that lies in the mountainous northeastern part of a larger region known as the Four Corners. Named after the spot where four states join, the region includes the southwestern mountains and semi-arid basins of Colorado, the canyon country of southeastern Utah, and the mountain, mesa and desert country of northwestern New Mexico and northeastern Arizona. This is an immense and wild region with incredibly diverse topography. It is also a region of incredible mineral and energy wealth. *Four Corners* is not just the name of the region, it is also the name of a coal-fired electric generating plant, one in a series of such plants that is reputed to be among the biggest emitters of sulfur dioxide in the world. Lime Creek, the aspen wood I so love to walk and the sky that illuminates them, all lie in the path of those emissions. A sky that Edward Abbey once called the last great clean air reservoir in the United States is now threatened by the energy needs of the Southwest. Just as the beauty of the great cathedrals of Europe is slowly eroding from sulfur dioxide pollution and associated acid rain, so is this forest which is the embodiment of their source and inspiration.

Once, as I stood in midstream fishing the lovely, flat glide of water that flows through the aspen wood, I heard a crashing and clanging that could only mean one thing: someone's horses were coming my way. As the crashing and clanging grew louder, the horses came into view. I recognized them at once. One, a muscular black gelding, was hobbled and struggling to move, his forelegs joined together by a leather strap designed to limit his range and make him easier to catch when needed. With him was a slender, tall roan mare wearing a collar with a large, loud bell. These were the favorite saddle- and packhorses of a man I knew well, a man I had worked with often. The horses had accompanied us on jobs as well as pleasure trips into the high country. With pack animals carrying a massive canvas sheepherder tent, woodstove, chainsaw, cots, heavy bedrolls, cast iron skillets and elk steaks, we had seemed to be making a mockery of all the spartan backpacking trips I have made without benefit of horses.

Perhaps these two, the black and the roan, had recognized my scent and come to say hello. After a few words of greeting, some affectionate nuzzling and flank thumping, they crashed and clanged off into the woods and left me to my fishing. Fishing, however, was no longer possible. I had been taken from my favorite place on my favorite stream and transported by the commotion of the horses to another, less pleasant place.

No one lives in Silverton and has the great luxury of free time to spend fishing Lime Creek without making a few compromises. That is, of course, unless that person is independently wealthy, which I am not. For several years I financed my life in the mountains with a job that took me away from the San Juans. In a stream of events that is still not clear to me, I once found myself leaving the employ of a gold mine near Silverton and driving off to work in the swamps of Texas as the newest member of a survey crew that was doing floodplain analysis, all on the basis of a handshake and a smile. The handshake and the smile came from the man who owned these horses.

He had hired me as the result of a conversation in a bar with a friend of mine. The friend, a woman I had worked with at a small publishing company a few years earlier, knew I was looking for a change in employment from my job as an underground mine electrician. The man had been drinking and spinning tales about wilderness surveying and rugged country. When he said he was looking for somebody who could read aerial photographs, my friend mentioned me. He called me from the bar that very night, not quite sober, mumbling about floodplain analysis, control surveying and stereo-photographs. He said he would come to see me in the morning.

I supposed that some drunk was indulging an amorous fantasy about my friend, and in the hope of expediting his plans and dreams for the evening, made up some tall tales about being a hotshot surveyor and got caught up in his lies to the point where he had to pretend to offer me a job. I never expected to see him. I certainly never expected what I met when I did see him, promptly as promised, the next day.

Rolling up to my house was a white pickup truck, a truck without a speck of dirt anywhere on its gleaming exterior after driving through the dusty unpaved streets of Silverton, a truck that literally bristled with long and short radio antennae. Out stepped a neatly dressed cowboy wearing a brand new black Resistol hat and carrying a briefcase. In the briefcase, which he opened upon entering the house, were topographical maps, computer printouts, a massive pile of aerial photographs of what looked to be rather unpleasant country, a Hewlett-Packard calculator, a dozen or so perfectly sharpened pencils and some field books. He spoke rapidly about needing someone who could interpret the photographs, do post-flight photo-identification, fill in as the crew artist (drawing bridges and other water-impeding structures) and maybe learn to survey so he could help with the fieldwork. He talked a lot about third-order-differential-leveling, one-in-50,000-horizontal-control and a million other things I hadn't the slightest knowledge of, then asked if I was the man for the job. I talked a bit, told him what I had done, what I hadn't and what I thought I could learn.

He looked me in the eye, smiled and said, "I guess you'll do." I asked him if he wanted to see a resume, and he laughed. "Those things are worthless" he said. "I'll know after I get you in the field if you're worth a damn." That day was the first of many in a seven-year career as a surveyor.

I was right about the photographs. The country was rather unpleasant. That first job involved six weeks of walking through swamps and bayous, dodging cottonmouths and utterly para-noid property owners in the sweltering lowlands of east Texas. In the course of six weeks we changed crews many times over, gaining and losing crew members as the heat, humidity and perfectionist demands of our cowboy boss conspired to wither surveyor after surveyor. At the end, only three remained: the cowboy, the Silvertonian and a brilliant mathematician pre-sumed by many of his hometown friends to be little more than a regular at the Hollywood Bar in Dolores, Colorado. After that the work got easier, and the bonds of friendship on our crew grew stronger.

We did resource analysis mapping for the forest service in the remarkably untouched Jemez Mountains of New Mexico. We did control surveys for power line right-of-ways in the McCullough Range of Nevada. We rode horses together, spent a lot of time walking the woods and a substantial part of our lives bouncing through rugged country in four-wheel-drive pickups. Almost always it was work that I loved, in the com-pany of men I greatly respected. It was also work constantly touched by the uneasiness of moral ambiguity. There was a pipeline survey for a geothermal project that dissected the flank of a mountain sacred to the Jemez Indians. There was a survey for a coal project that threatened to destroy the delicate masonry of the ancient outlier communities of the Chaco Canyon Anasazi sites. There was always a justification of some kind—sometimes a job for a strip mine meant establishing of existing surface contours so the land could be reclaimed to resemble the original topography after mining had been completed—but such rationalization never completely assuaged my fear that I was involved in something that was fundamentally wrong.

In these parts there is a bumper sticker that is quite common. It reads: Ban Mining, Let the Bastards Freeze in the Dark! I think of it often when I get on my environmental high horse. I like my Fiberglass skis, my graphite fly rods and the technology that has made them possible. I have grown accustomed to letting electric heaters take up the slack from the wood stove on cold winter nights. Still, it bothers me to dig up the land I love and leave it lying in ruin, whether it has been restored to original contours or not, even if the item extracted is for ski edges, fly rods, the coal to make electricity for my home, or something else I use. There is an inconsistency here, and anyone who claims not to be a part of it is a fool.

George Sibley, a great regional writer of the West, once commented on the irony apparent in the holy and uncompromising environmental activist words he shared with another writer as they flew to an environmental conference in Denver, all the while spilling the waste of diesel-fueled jet engines in the pristine air of their profoundly loved western skies. Sibley asked the other activist if this bothered him. The activist had no idea what he was talking about. He refused to see himself as part of the problem. Sibley's feelings about the environmental movement became a bit confused after that encounter, as have mine after similar incidents.

My uneasiness about the moral inconsistencies between my occupation and my love of the land mounted until I wore it on each job as part of my costume. Its presence became as accepted and familiar as my own black Resistol hat, surveyor's vest, field book and gnat bites.

Perhaps the ultimate irony was the assignment to do a job on the coalfields that fed the Navajo generator, one of those in the series of plants near the Four Corners that create the pollution that threatens my home and Lime Creek. We were to do a surface contour survey that would aid in reclamation after mining was completed. The mathematician and I were to run differential levels through an undisturbed area by starting from a point of known elevation and working to another point of known elevation, establishing reference points along the way. Our work area lay adjacent to a large pit that was being worked by one of the mine's mammoth draglines. The cowboy would do the horizontal survey by himself, and we would combine the data to produce the final report.

We were working on a piece of land that, as yet, lay outside of the actual mining area. As we worked we could hear distant sirens that indicated an imminent blast, a warning meant to keep people from inadvertently walking into an area that was about to explode.

Blasting at the mine was done to loosen the overburden, the soil that lies on top of the coal seam, so it can be easily removed. Such blasting involves the drilling of holes through the overburden, perhaps 40 or 50 feet deep, and filling them with explosives. An area the size of the next pit to be worked, perhaps 40 acres at a time, is blown with a single detonation. The resulting blast is unimaginably large. To walk into one at the wrong time means certain death. Hence the sirens.

As we worked toward our closing benchmark the sirens grew louder and it dawned on us that something was wrong. No one else could be seen in our area. Worse, we noticed that some of the spectators who had come to see the explosion were standing on bluffs behind us. We were between these spectators and the sirens. We had been told that if we did not walk *through* sounding sirens, we would be safe, but as we got closer to the sound we realized that we had come into the mine from a route outside of the mine property and not one that the safety officers were used to protecting. Danny, the mathematician, a

wise man and Vietnam vet with a keen nose for danger, lit a cigarette and suggested we wait awhile before going any farther.

After a few minutes the sirens changed from a steady wail
to a frantic warbling. Then all hell broke loose. We saw the
ground about a quarter mile in front of us heave and fly above
us into the air. Then a fireball exploded, filling the sky with
orange light, and there was the sound of an explosion that
pounded our chests with the strength of a sledgehammer. The
earth, which had been lifted so violently into the sky, returned
with a whistling sound and began to fall around us. I was
riveted to my place, frozen as I had been as a child in terrifying
dreams, knowing that I had to find cover, unable to close my
mouth or move. I thought, in a moment that lasted forever, of
something my father had said when telling stories about his
exploits on the Pacific islands in World War II. My friends and
I had been playing war, throwing clods of dirt into the air and
whistling as they came down and exploded on the ground. He
had said that you didn't have to worry about the shells that
whistled. It was the ones that whooshed that got you. I heard
a whooshing in the air. It grew louder. Still riveted in place, I
watched a chunk of earth the size of an automobile smash into
the ground not 10 feet from where I stood, its impact blasting
me out of my paralysis. I turned around and looked for Danny.
He had disappeared. Running, I dove into a small culvert
behind me and found Danny, whose instincts had placed him
there centuries or seconds ago. He was curled up in a fetal
position, his hands hugging his hard hat for all he was worth.

When the last piece of blasted earth had settled, we emerged
from our hole frightened and feeling very lucky to be alive. We
rarely took breaks while working, but we took one that day. We
sat on the ground. We trembled. We did not speak. Danny lit
another cigarette. I, who was trying to quit smoking, bummed
one from Danny without regret and joined him in a smoke.
When the cigarettes were done we resumed our line of levels,

not speaking until the job was completed. When the pickup man came to get us at the end of our day in the field, he was animated and excited. He spoke rapidly about the incredible blast he had seen and asked if we had been able to see it. Danny and I looked at each other and allowed as how we had.

Before we left the mine Danny and I took a trip into the pits to see close up the machines that dredged the coal from the earth. We walked the road toward the pits and watched the shovels grow larger. From a distance of about a mile, they appear to be something like ordinary steam shovels, but as the distance decreases their actual size becomes apparent. These are no ordinary shovels. Up close they look like something from a movie too fantastic to be believed, something Steven Spielberg might dream about after eating too much pizza. They sit before you more like huge buildings than machines. They climb nine stories into the air. They drag thousands of tons of earth with indescribable ease. They move, these nine-story buildings, silently, efficiently, constantly. We watched them, unable to believe what we saw, unable to find a perspective or scale that made sense out of the sight. It seemed as if a handful of these machines, and there are many of them working the coal seams of the West, could eat the entire earth with little trouble, given a few weeks.

Most of the workers in this mine come from the surrounding communities and isolated homes of the Navajo reservation on which the mines and power plants sit. The chronically poor reservations welcomed the coming of energy development on their lands and the jobs that development would create. As I looked at the strobe lights flashing on a shovel's towering arm and gazed into the distance toward the massive stacks of the power plant also covered with these same brilliant lights, I wondered, How good will these jobs seem a few years down the road when the coal is gone, the land has been changed and the sky, which once was pure and filled this land with a magical light, is dimmed forever?

Native Americans have many legends and stories that describe and explain, entertain and teach about the relationship between man and the land. Among them are the coyote tales that depict the coyote as a foolish but cunning deceiver. The laughter that erupted from our mouths was both sad and acutely ironic as we walked around the giant shovel and saw a huge coyote painted on its constantly pivoting, always working back. This coyote was not the cunning deceiver of the old stories, he was the coyote of modern America, the always defeated, pathetic beast of the Saturday morning cartoon shows.

Back at Lime Creek, still standing in the stream, the horses gone, I looked at the deep blue sky and the light in the aspen wood and wondered again. How long will it be before my cathedral is lost to the excesses and deceptions of economic development, excesses and deceptions whose source lies partly in the desire for a better life, but more often in the exploitation of that hope by those whose only motivation is the dark selfishness of greed? How long before we realize that the energy waste and opulence that characterize our lives can be supported only temporarily, even by the vast reserves of coal that lie beneath the land of the West? Coyote must wonder as well. Miners paint his face on their machines, thinking of the modern diversions of television and Saturday mornings, not of the centuries-old legends that taught us about the land. Coyote taught through cunning, but his deceptions and tricks always left behind something good. A laugh. A lesson. What will be left when the sky above Lime Creek has been stolen?

The
Fisher
and the Marten

3

There was a time when I would tell people that I was going fishing, even if I was not, because it seemed that fishing is a vastly more acceptable pastime for an adult than walking the woods alone. This is especially true when the need to be alone in the woods has become something of a mania—a preoccupation that has replaced the desire to work, the need for human companionship and any desire for civilized amenities or other supposedly more constructive behaviors. In the San Juans a person who likes to spend time alone is accepted, but seen as a bit strange. A person who likes to spend time alone in the woods appears a bit stranger and is seen, perhaps, as being a little weird. But a guy who is going fishing, even if he does little else and is always alone, is thought to be just fine. Fishing is a madness that is understood. Maybe this is because so many San Juaners spend so much time fishing that if it were seen any other way we might have to admit to harboring more than our share of sociopaths, and who wants to admit to that? Besides, definitions of what may or may not be normal are statistical not absolute, and numbers (in the San Juans at any rate) would seem to indicate that not fishing would make one vastly less normal than having the desire to leave hearth and home for days on end to sleep on the cold ground, all the while avoiding human contact like the plague (spies might discover one of your secret hot spots!), in order to stand for hours in cold water chasing the elusive lunker trout. This behavior, strange as it might seem elsewhere, is actually quite common here in the San Juans. After years of pretense, years of saying I was going fishing when all I really wanted was some time alone in the woods, I am happy to report that I have finally become practically normal. Now when I say I'm going fishing that is just what I intend to do.

Fishing is perhaps too broad a term. My personal route to normalcy is the desire to fly-fish in streams for trout. This particular manifestation of the norm might be a bit difficult for the outsider or the uninitiated to understand, so in the interest of clarity I will try to describe it.

The dedicated trout fly-fisher will try to divide his time roughly as follows:

On working days (those rare days away from the stream) he will spend about eight hours at his job, eight hours sleeping, two hours preparing and eating food, an hour in travel between home and work (depending on where he lives and works) and five hours preparing tackle, tying flies, fondling a favorite rod, staring into fly-boxes or reading fishing books. He will think about fishing for roughly 22 hours, which includes daydreaming at work and night dreaming at home. The rest of his thought-time is divided between noble aspirations (Has anyone ever been awarded a Nobel Prize for inventing a new fly pattern? Could I be the first?), mundane details (Was I supposed to take my son to the orthodontist yesterday?) and wondering if he remembered to shut off the stove burner before he carried his dinner into the study where he spent the evening tying those previously mentioned flies.

You may wonder, if he is married and has children, when is there time for a fisherman to be with or think about them? So do his wife and children. But if he is lucky enough to have a wife and if he has been able to maintain a truly American home that espouses traditional values (i.e., the wife does all the work), he will have an additional two hours to fondle rods, tie flies, stare at fly boxes, etc., because he will be spared the drudgery of preparing meals, doing laundry, making beds and other time-consuming tasks. Married or not, any time spent cleaning is spent polishing the ferrules and glowing bamboo of that favorite split-cane fly rod (an elegant nine-foot-long, three-and-a-half-ounce will-o'-the-wisp that inspires as much affection, maybe more, as the trout). If he is really dedicated he will try to arrange it so that none of these days (workdays, that is) occur during the fishing season, which runs from July through November here in the mountains and can be extended from January through December with judiciously selected trips to nearby areas with good spring and winter fishing.

Fishing days are spent fishing, eating and sleeping. Period. The only other diversion is occasionally wondering why, on those dreadful days when he wasn't fishing, he didn't spend *even more* time preparing tackle, tying flies and staring at fly boxes to figure out what flies he actually needed.

Money is apportioned in a similar fashion. Tackle is paramount, food secondary, rent or mortgage payments transcendental and therefore of no consequence. Clothing is very important. Waders, fishing vests and such are always in the best of repair and the finest that can be purchased. Underwear is another matter entirely. My mother used to tell me that I should pay special attention to the condition and cleanliness of my underwear in case I should be hit by a truck, God forbid, and have to go to the hospital. What a horrible embarrassment it would be to overhear a prep-nurse commenting about the sorry state of my underwear as I faded from consciousness on the way to surgery. Most fly-fishermen I know better not get hit by a truck. Their mothers would never forgive them.

I avow that this description of the dedicated fly-fisherman

is fairly accurate. I also maintain that I am not quite as dedicated as some and therefore not so completely divorced from other aspects of reality as the fisherman described above. I do spend time with my family and perhaps a bit more time working. My better half, I think, would have argued that I once was a bit more dedicated to fishing than I realized, and that I was, therefore, closer to being the physical embodiment of this description than I knew. I thank her for having seen me as being, well, so nearly normal.

Lime Creek, as you may guess, is a superb trout stream. The foregoing description of a fisherman may have been a bit of an exaggeration, but it is definitely true that I was considered a bit strange when I was spending a great deal of time alone in the woods, and also true that I am perhaps considered a bit less strange now that I spend much of that time fishing. If you suspect that I spend a great deal of time fishing Lime Creek, you are right. As much as I love the Lime Creek valley and as much as I love fly-fishing, wedding the two loves was as natural for me as love itself.

Fishing stories of the "How I Caught the Twenty-Nine Pound Brown Trout Who Was So Smart We All Called Him Einstein" type bore me. I know enough to be bored because I've seen more than a few of my friends fall asleep as I've tried to tell some such story of my own. In truth, the conquests made by fishermen are never quite as interesting to me as stories about the conquering of the fishermen themselves. By fish. By streams. By the experience of being in the woods with fishing rods. This story will, I hope, fall into this second category.

Tellers of fishing stories are always making up phony names for their favorite streams to protect them from discovery, or downplaying the quality of fishing to keep others away. Some people will probably be furious with me for revealing the whereabouts of such great fishing, just as friends have chided me for singing the praises of the San Juans in other books and articles. I plead the happy insanity of a man in love with a place. In addition, I must confess that I have not yet lost all faith in my fellow man. Somehow I am not yet fearful that either the San Juans or Lime Creek will be overrun with hordes of insensitive, noisy, beer-can slinging invaders. I hope I'm not wrong. It doesn't seem to me that the subtleties of Lime Creek would attract or hold for long anyone who would destroy it, and the experience of these subtleties might greatly enrich the lives of those who get to know the valley. Who am I to keep all this to myself?

The trout in Lime Creek come from many different populations. Most are wild. Some are stocked. The stocked trout are at a distinct disadvantage in the creek's fast water and difficult conditions. Few, it seems, make it through too many winters. Most succumb to baited hooks, lures or flies, or fail to reproduce and die without progeny. The few stocked fish who do survive long enough to reproduce have the genetic moxie to ensure that the wild populations that result from their breeding success will continue to make it and continue to adapt to their surroundings. They will, in effect, become truly wild.

The wild fish whose ancestral roots began in a fish hatchery inhabit the lower stretches of the creek. Here, there are a few brown trout, which were brought to this country from their native Europe. There are a great many brook trout, which were originally found in the streams and lakes of eastern North America. Although most are small, some achieve monumental proportions for mountain stream brookies (nine to 10 inches) and a brilliance of color and scrappiness when hooked that inspires admiration. Wild populations of rainbow trout, which are native to the West Coast of North America, also inhabit the stream. These acrobatic leapers would seem to be the favorites of anglers. They grow larger than brookies, fight splendidly and are not quite so hard to catch as brown trout, which quickly

45

become wary after exposure to angling. Finally there are the true natives of Lime Creek: cutthroat trout. These trout, threatened throughout their range by interbreeding with introduced trout, environmental degradation and the hard knocks of trout life, appear to be thriving in the upper reaches of Lime Creek. They are protected from genetic disaster by the physical barriers of a topography that keeps away stocked fish and introduced wild populations, protected from anglers by the relatively rough country and, so far at least, protected from environmental degradation by the pristine and natural environment through which Lime Creek's headwaters flow. If there is one fish that represents the angling soul of the San Juans, it has to be the Lime Creek cutthroat.

I would be lying if I were to say that fishing for cutthroat trout can be done without mixed emotions. I have done it for a great variety of reasons. One was simply to get food, although I no longer keep cutthroats, preferring to fish for food among the less precious and rare species. Another reason has been to reassure myself that they remain in the watershed. Each year, after the long winter, I find myself consumed with the fear that they might have been wiped out in the bitter cold. I am unable to relax until a good day of fishing near treeline has reassured me that the population remains alive and well. So far, each spring this has proven to be the case. Still, I would have to be fairly insensitive or uncaring to think that the act of putting a hook, even a barbless one, in the lip of a trout is a matter of no consequence that involves no responsibility. A choice to act in this way can be made in ignorance. Many fishermen, I think, fish in such an envelope of arrogance. Many more grapple with the conflict between their passion for fishing and their legitimate love of their quarry, and in so doing find resolution for issues that transcend the mere act of fishing.

To resolve the conflict in a place like the Lime Creek valley, with a fish as noble as the Lime Creek cutthroat, makes the resolution somehow more profound and the lessons learned perhaps more significant than what could be achieved in the midst of civilization or on a trout stream unlike this one. This stream has likely changed little since the retreat of the glaciers at the end of the last ice age. It has seen and been seen by nomadic hunter-gatherers. Today it is a place that can provide continuity between us and those who hunted here long ago. It can also help us understand the biological inheritance they bequeathed to us.

When I fish the creek I often become lost in the concentration required to find, stalk and induce a trout to take a fly. There is water to read and wade safely. There are trout to locate and somehow not frighten. A decision must be made about what insect might appeal to the fish and what fly might successfully imitate it. Finally there is the cast, and if all goes well, the rise, the setting of the hook, the playing and releasing, or the solemn matter of killing the fish so that it can be eaten later.

Sometimes the concentration becomes so intense that hours pass with little notice of anything beyond the watery world of the creek. I have been startled out of this mental isolation by many things. Water ouzels have flashed past me, landing midstream on rocks where they peep their distinctive call and dip their tails in characteristic fashion. Once an eagle buzzed me in a way that made me wonder if he had decided only at the last minute that I might prove too heavy to carry off as dinner. Sometimes the light has changed dramatically, suddenly glowing a brilliant red on the summits of surrounding mountains as twilight gathered, and I have been left staring in midstream, my line trailing uselessly in the current, struck dumb by the awesome beauty of mountain light. More times than I care to remember my concentration has been broken by the sudden discovery that I have stepped into a hole deeper than my waders or over my head, and I have sputtered, wallowed and floundered to shore, having gone quickly from the bliss of reverie to the violent shaking and panting that come after an unexpected fall into frigid water. Never, however, has any event startled me as much as the protestations of a pine marten that assaulted me verbally from streamside when he came upon me standing in midstream, lost in concentration.

The marten had come to the stream for whatever reason martens come to streams. He certainly had not come to see me. I first became aware of him when I heard a hideous hissing. Looking in the direction of the noise I saw him jumping up and down on a large flat rock, baring his pointed teeth in a ferocious display. Clearly he was angry. After a few minutes of this he ran off into the streamside willows, but returned minutes later to resume his display. His anger was obviously directed at me and his behavior exhibited no fear. He seemed to view me as a rival. He wanted me out of his territory. What we had here was a battle for turf. Without thinking, I bared my teeth, stared him in the eye and began hissing and jumping myself. After a few seconds of this he ran off and did not return.

After his departure I sat on his streamside rock and wondered, What the hell kind of behavior was that from a supposedly intelligent being? What had happened to reverie and compassion and empathy? Why had I acted so strangely? What right had I to interfere with this natural being trying to protect his territory? Thank God no one had seen me! How would I ever have explained that display? More important, how would I ever explain it to myself?

How do I explain that I fish for and sometimes kill creatures I profess to love, living things that fill me with wonder and affection? Questions like this often lead people toward vegetarianism. I have a friend who says she does not eat anything that would try to run away. Are vegetables fair game because they cannot run? Do they die any less than animals when we cook and eat them?

The Fisher and the Marten

Any creature that eats to stay alive must live from the death of others, whether they be plant or animal. That someone else does the killing for us in most cases does not relieve us of responsibility. If we view this killing as murder, we must either sanction murder or commit suicide through malnutrition. Few of us choose death and few of us sanction murder. Where is the resolution of this conflict?

The resolution lies, I think, in the realization that life and death are natural events. One creature's death as food for another involves a gift, that if not willingly given should at the very least be gratefully received. If there is no gratitude for this gift, then life is indeed cruel and brutal. If, however, the acceptance of this gift is seen as a celebration of life, if one realizes that ultimately one's own death will feed the earth and sustain life—if only as fertilizer—then there is a wholeness to the cycle. A sense of belonging to the natural world and an acceptance of death, our own and that of other beings, that can never be achieved in denial.

When I fish and do not kill, I sharpen my skills and my insight. I believe that prehistoric hunters occasionally did the same. The fish I catch and release are, hopefully, less likely to be caught in the future. When I fish and kill, I do so with gratitude. I thank the fish for its flesh and I try to kill it quickly and with as little suffering as possible. This behavior was foreign to me before I fished Lime Creek.

A large part of my learning about food, and the roles of the hunter and the hunted, was crystalized in my encounter with the marten and in my strangely instinctive response to his display. The marten challenged me in a battle for territory. Lost in my hunt, having no time to think, I responded as a hunter and answered his challenge. On that day and in that battle, the challenger backed down. I know that it will not always be so.

Lime Creek

On
Being Human

4

Orion swung across the wind-
shield, repeatedly traversing the space from left to right and
back, sweeping the star-specked expanse above me as I drove
the tortuous highway that parallels Lime Creek. The night
glowed with the bright light of stars in the clear sky of high
altitude. There were an unknowable number of brilliant, flick-
ering, gemlike points of light in that winter sky, but Orion
dominated the scene. He seemed not merely to be hunting the
Great Bear; rather, he appeared to be in total control of the
night. The stars, planets, galaxies and nebulae, the constella-
tions that mankind began to see in the deep fullness of the
firmament when we inhabited it with our own realities, the
mythologies with which we populated it as we articulated our
self-awareness and began to create our history as a race—all
seemed subservient to the giant figure of the hunter. Orion
ruled the night sky, a representation of man in the cosmos, the
emblem of our dreams and illusions.

The horizon before me was a jagged black line, a line that
defined the incredible bulk of the mountains. Below it nothing
could be seen but indecipherable blackness. Below this mass of
black, between the sky and me, lay what appeared to be a

bottomless abyss. The abyss, that night, was Lime Creek.

I was driving home from the hospital in Durango for the third night in a row. I was fighting fatigue. I was fighting fear. I was fighting a grief the likes of which I had never known. K.B. had been diagnosed as having acute myelogenous leukemia three days before. I was told by the doctors to face squarely the reality that she could easily die within six weeks, and if lucky enough to have a remission, would probably relapse and die within a year or two. They spoke to us together. Gently. They spoke to me alone. More bluntly. Always the message was the same. There is a chance to prolong life, but we must realize the seriousness of the situation. Karen and I needed to get our affairs in order.

When they spoke during those first days of the illness, the words always seemed to be floating from their mouths. They emerged in slow motion, visible and framed in balloons, the balloons of cartoon characters. Whenever they were there, whenever we sat in a small group of three or four—Karen, one or two doctors and me—I viewed the room from a distance, from another place. I looked at the scene not as a participant, but as if I had floated off, or more accurately, as if I had stumbled onto a group of strangers and stayed, hidden in a corner of the room, to watch and listen as the tragic events unfolded. None of it could be fathomed. None of it made sense. As the days passed, gradual realization gouged a hole in the cavity that once had been my chest. My organs disappeared, and in their place an empty space grew where once my heart had been. The space, the emptiness, became larger every day. It ached most as I drove home along Lime Creek and as I lay in bed trying to sleep, aware as never before of the bloated fullness and pain an emptiness can create. My beloved K.B. was dying.

Many of my years in the San Juans have been spent alone, and for most of that time I believed that was exactly how I preferred to be. Fortunately, I had also discovered that strong friendships could be forged on the basis of a shared love of the mountains, and I spent many good times in the woods with others. I also knew that it would have been foolhardy to have climbed or skied alone in the backcountry. Nonetheless, there were days, weeks and months when I had no serious contact with another person.

My various jobs also involved a great deal of freedom; indeed, I had arranged it that way. My graphic arts work for a local publisher was undertaken with the clear understanding that I would meet whatever deadlines were necessary, but on my terms. I would work late at night when a beautiful day called me to the trout stream. I would take several days off for a climbing trip in the middle of the week, then make up the work over a weekend. I would go to New Mexico for a two-week survey job because I knew that the work would earn me enough money to take a month off to be alone in the hills. This, I assured myself, was living.

For several years, when I was at home, winter found skis and a loaded pack by my door at all times, while summer found a totally self-contained backpack in the same spot. If I was not out in the woods, I was preparing to go. The rest of life, it seemed, supported the time in the backcountry, and nothing else seemed quite so real, or so much like *living*. I had a great deal of difficulty understanding the concerns of those who worked regular hours, vacationed two weeks a year and spent 50 weeks wishing they were somewhere else. These seemed to be the only options: freedom or slavery. Security was bought only at the expense of happiness, with a real job, a regular schedule, apparent stability and unavoidable misery.

Even more frightening than a real job was a permanent relationship. Certainly such a relationship would create bonds that would be as damaging to this carefully constructed life of freedom as any commitment to a real job. Such a relationship might even prove more damaging than any employment scenario. Relationships involve emotional bonds that are infinitely more complex than any that exist between an employer and an employee. I didn't know it at the time, but my freedom had been gained at a price far higher than the loss of financial security. I had encumbered myself with a limited view of freedom and in the process had arrested my progress as a human being.

This may seem like an odd time to make such a confession, but this is a book about place and about Lime Creek in particular. An exploration of place cannot be made apart from the realization of our humanity. We make a grave mistake when we assume that it is possible for a person to become invisible, to cease to be human and to experience a place as if he or she were a disembodied being. All too many of us make the mistake of attempting just that, and I suspect that many who do are people who have been alone too long. A lot, it seems, are nature writers.

It is easy to imagine that we do not exist, that we blend into the scenery as easily as another aspen in the grove, when there is no one around to remind us of our true nature. Without the reminder, we tend to forget there is a difference between being human and being something else. I know this may be hard for some to believe. Where is there evidence of such a mistake? Who has ever confused his own being with that of other natural creatures? Well, I for one have done it. I have read many books by naturalists who have spent time alone in the woods and made the same mistake. I have spoken with others. More seriously in error (and perhaps more common) are those who fall prey to the uniquely human foible of wishing to be something other than what they are—a response often rooted in the belief that people are somehow *unnatural*. I have heard many express the desire to be a tree or a bird, anything but human. I suppose I should just laugh and enjoy the irony of the wish, the humor in this all-too-human trait. Can you imagine a lion wishing to be a whale, a blade of grass wanting to be a bird? No other creature would be so stupid as to imagine itself unnatural or wish to be something else. I guess we humans have a wide range of options, good and bad.

As much as I love to be alone in the woods or to share the woods with friends, I have found a special joy in being out with someone I love, someone with whom the distinction between individual destinies has become blurred until there is a deeply held belief that the destiny we share is one. This joy came to me with Karen's arrival in the San Juans. My realization of the inescapability and inevitability of my humanness also came with her arrival. I had walked the woods and stalked the trout, smelled the dirt and learned much before she came, but I had walked and stalked and learned little of the creature and the paths within me and little of what it means to be a human in the woods.

When Karen arrived her knowledge of plants and wildlife was mostly limited to those of the eastern states, and in the beginning I taught with great authority and pomposity about our western species and ecology. It didn't take me long to see that her special sensitivity to flora easily and profoundly eclipsed my own. Within a matter of months it was she who was teaching, with considerably more grace, might I add, than I had been able to muster. Her ability to handle any fear of heights on the exposed ridges of high mountains was greater than I had expected, and I found myself calling her "the mountain goat." We hiked and climbed a great deal together, initially following my attraction toward these high, exposed places. Her true love, however, was the wooded place, not the sparseness of tundra and high crags. In her company I soon learned much about the joy to be found in the quiet places I had previously passed through en route to something higher up.

LIME CREEK ODYSSEY

We spent much time together in Lime Creek. Sometimes we would walk the bank together. Other times she would wade behind me as I fished upstream. Many days we would arrive at the creek, I would don my fishing clothes and we would part. I would fish, knowing she was roaming the woods above me, and she would hike, aware of my presence below. My memories of those days with K.B. are as vivid as any I possess, and as full of warmth and happiness as any person might conceive.

One afternoon we hiked a long stretch of the valley far below a section of the old road known by locals as the Chinese Wall. The road, which edges along the flanks of Spud Mountain high above the creek, consists at this spot of a narrow dirt track with stonework barricades placed between travelers and the chasm below. The regularly spaced four-foot-high masonry blocks give the road an appearance very much like that of the Great Wall of China, hence the name. At one point on our hike, K.B. and I needed to cross the stream. Each of us, being bull-headed and independent, chose a separate path. K.B.'s path, several hundred yards upstream from my own, involved straddling a log that hung over a deep, cold pool. As she crossed, her dangling legs caught enough current to flip her off the log and into the water. I heard her screaming, and when I finally got to her, she was shivering on the bank, her clothes utterly soaked with the icy water of the creek. As she began to remove her wet garments, I offered her a dry jacket that I was carrying in my pack. Just as she pulled off her last piece of clothing, a fisherman who had been upstream came to see what the commotion was all about. We found ourselves frantically trying to maintain some sense of decency by covering up the most embarrassing portions of her exposed anatomy before he emerged into view from the brush. When he left, we resumed the drying process and laughed ourselves silly at the absurdity of the situation.

On another occasion Karen sat on a rock by the stream, her

face lowered to its surface to observe the ants who toiled there. I waded upstream to fish, and held each trout above water to show to her before it was released. I didn't know that her attention was so focused on the ants that she didn't see any of the fish I so proudly offered for inspection. She also failed to see when, stalking a large rainbow, I stepped into a deep, fast-running glide that carried me away, my waders filling rapidly with frigid water. I emerged from the stream sputtering and shivering, chilled to the bone, and joined her on the rock. This time it was my turn to take off my clothes and warm up. Again we laughed until it hurt.

Many times we removed our clothes together, even though neither of us had fallen into the creek, to make love in an open meadow under the warmth of the sun or in the broken light of a glowing wood beside the noisy water of our favorite stream.

One day, during the fall before she fell ill, we hiked into the canyon together, examining plants, holding them and each other, walking, sometimes speaking, sometimes silent. At one point we traversed across loose rock on a steep slope above the stream. I watched from behind as K.B. expertly and gracefully moved across the slope. Her progress was steadied by her ice axe, which she had grown so attached to she would not hike without it. I watched her walk across the scene—creek below, deep blue sky above, mountains and forest all around—and was so filled with love and joy that I was overwhelmed with emotion.

Now she was in the hospital. As I passed the valley on my way home, the great pleasure of those moments turned into a sadness I could hardly stand. How would I ever be able to be there again, once she had gone?

For readers of the philosophical literature relating to nature and man's place within it, the foregoing must seem to embody all that is wrong with our attitudes about the earth. It reeks of anthropocentrism; that is, it regards nature in terms of man and his experiences. It makes man central in the understanding of nature. In the current debate no word is as ugly as *anthropocentrism*, and no epithet as condemnatory. Still, anyone who would deny the validity of feelings like those I felt at Lime Creek, in the hope of maintaining philosophical purity, is worse than a fool; he is a liar. The person who feels no love, who does not experience nature and place with and through his love of others, is either dead, or perhaps more sadly, alone. There must be a difference between the arrogant anthropocentrism that gives us the feeling that the world is ours to use, and a gentler but still uniquely human response that allows us to experience the world through the special position of our very real and undeniable humanity. Otherwise, we would have to argue that there is no difference between exploitation and love, and I believe them to be polar opposites.

The strong position taken against anthropocentrism is understandable. Historically, the belief that man is central in the universe has yielded some rather disastrous results. Its roots lie most identifiably in a theism that sees mankind as the reflection of God on earth and therefore sees men as the lords of creation. It has taken several thousand years to go from this position to that of a contemporary belief, espoused by men such as James Watt, that natural resources *ought* to be used up by man because that is why they are there. The logic behind this thought transition is not so stretched as to do a disservice to the original premise. If man is the reflection of God on earth and if we are the lords of creation, then the world is, indeed, here for our use. This, to me, is ugly anthropocentrism.

It is also understandable that many, repulsed by this position and by the destruction of habitat and the killing of non-human species that have been justified with such premises, would draw back in horror and embarrassment of their own humanity and the havoc that mankind has wrought. For these people, anthropocentrism is repudiated by the extreme response of believing man to be not just less than central, but peripheral. Man is an unnecessary and evil component of the natural world. Not only is man not better than the grasses, trees, squirrels and bears, he is infinitely worse. In response to their embarrassment, these people recoil in horror from their humanness and repudiate everything they feel to be human.

When this second position is taken, there are results that are as disastrous, I fear, as rampant exploitation of the world and its non-human creatures. In denying the very real aspects of our lives and the perceptions that make us human, we ask for nothing less than the ability to transcend nature. Once again we are wanting to be better than the rest of the world. In our attempt to run from arrogance, we have reaffirmed it. The only legitimate position is one of neither arrogance nor shame, it is one of acceptance and a search for legitimate responses to the undeniable fact of our humanness and our existence within the natural world.

To write about Lime Creek objectively, some would argue, I would have to divorce my observations from my emotions. It is true that I associate the valley with my love of mountains and streams and trout fishing, my knowing the valley through experiences in the company of friends and alone, and my learning about sharing a life and a destiny with another human being. All these things could be said to color and render useless my observations. This, some argue, is the difference between science and literature. Science observes impartially and accurately, literature with undeniable color but little reliability. Anyone familiar with the philosophy of science knows the folly of this assumption, but the illusion persists: there is objective observation and there is subjective observation. The objective observer somehow escapes the confines of his humanity. He becomes godlike: all seeing, all knowing, able to be in the world without influencing it or being influenced by it. This is sheer poppycock. To deny the power of experience to color perception, to deny the inevitability of its doing so, is to deny something fundamental to our humanity. It is as foolish for us to want this as it is for a worm to wish to become a bird. It is, in fact, unnatural.

There are undeniable differences between people and other creatures. It is our job, in the words of Goethe, to "become what we are." The defining and articulating of this involves a breadth of experience and wisdom that I do not presume to possess. I think I have a few hints about some of the possibilities, though.

To be people acting within nature surely means realizing and accepting that we are a part of nature, neither better nor worse than any other part. Recognizing our humanity involves our awareness of language, our sense of time and our tendency to ponder and reflect. These very human traits lead to something that Heidegger called "worlding the world"; that is, allowing other beings to be what they are, to witness what we and they do, and to create history by remembering and continuing the events in oral and written tradition. It means recognizing the existence within man of moral imperatives that influence behavior as much as other imperatives. This moral framework, I believe, is no less biological and adaptive in man than his patterns of procreation, hunting and cultivation. It means realizing that our subjective, colored observations can have profound meaning and reliability because we are, indeed, natural creatures. We feel and act the way we do because we have existed within and been affected by the natural world for millions of years. We are legitimately connected and therefore have nothing to fear but our strangely irrational desire to separate ourselves from nature. I haven't the foggiest idea where that desire came from or what purpose it serves. I suspect, however, that it, like all maladaptive behaviors, will be short lived.

On Being Human

As the weeks of K.B.'s illness passed and turned into months, the grief and agony, the shock of the original situation gradually gave way to the hope and fullness of life that are characteristic of a battle one wants very desperately to win. No small measure of this hope and fullness came from the strength and courage Karen showed in the face of horrible odds. Some, we were told, would die within weeks. Of those who survived the first weeks, only one in five would be cured. The rest would eventually relapse and die.

Life for K.B. meant being a constructive person, not one who took without giving back. Her approach to her illness was characterized by this attitude. All through her difficult struggle, she had the strength and the will to think about others and to continue the life she had lived before her illness. She could not die, she would not die, because she was not yet ready. She still had too much to do. Even in desperate illness she refused to become, as she used to say a "sludge on society."

After many days in the Durango hospital and several painful and difficult periods that involved massive doses of chemotherapy, terrible infections and repeated blood transfusions, it became obvious that Karen's only chance for a cure would be a bone-marrow transplant. Again, the odds were poor, and we knew that the process would be extremely difficult, but it was a choice she made readily. She was still not ready to die.

The illness and its treatment dominated the better part of a year, and in that time we saw precious little of Lime Creek and far too much of the hospital. The transplant took place in Los Angeles and took us away from our home in the San Juans for over two months. When we got back, Orion was no longer dominant in the sky above our heads. Winter had let go of the mountains. In its place, spring had come. The snows had gone in the torrent of the thaw. Lime Creek had carried away the deluge, and as the waters subsided, summer too had come and gone. When first we saw our mountain sky again, Orion was stalking along its edges and the Great Bear he pursued had ascended to prominence. I no longer saw Orion as a representation of human arrogance in the naming and understanding of nature. Orion the hunter, I realized, is a legitimate embodiment of man's "worlding the world," not in arrogance, but in the humble acceptance of wishing to be fully human, a wish that is felt only in the company of profound respect and love for all that is natural, including humans.

Lime Creek was one of the first places we visited when we returned from California. Karen had no hair, little strength and an assortment of medical difficulties that would have confined most people to bed, but the attraction of the woods was too strong to be resisted, and the clear low water of autumn murmured an irresistible invitation. We spent one glorious fall day there. It is a day I will always cherish, in a place that will always be filled with memories. I know it is foolish to associate a place so completely with another person. I know that I will pass, that glaciers and upheavals may well come and alter the stream forever, making my memories meaningless. I know that my limited associations and perspective mean little in the long term, but for now it is right and proper for me to see with my all-too-limited human eyes. To feel with my all-too-romantic human heart. To remember what I must. To be what I am is what any natural creature must do: bear, elk, deer, squirrel; eagle, falcon, jay, ouzel; pine, fir, willow; grasses; fish; insects; the very soil from which they all spring; and the stream which waters them. I am no less natural than they.

Thoughts from the Real World

5

All this talk about nature bothers a lot of city folks, and it wasn't until recently that it struck me what the problem was. Too many nature writers sound like a cross between Huck Finn and John Boy (I suppose I'm sometimes guilty of that myself), and by golly, there aren't too many city folks who talk like that. There is a suspicion among our urban brethren that all of this stuff about rapture in the woods is made up. If it isn't made up, then it just doesn't refer to anything in the real world. The real world has junkies and muggers and maybe just a few white collar criminals. Not much cause for rapture there. The woods have chipmunks that look suspiciously like Chip and Dale and act too much like Disney caricatures for their own damn good. Let's face it. Nature just ain't natural.

As unreal as nature seems to be, rural people (that is, people surrounded by nature) are infinitely more so. All those clean-faced and bright-eyed people sittin' around contemplating the meaning of life while worms get drowned on the end of their hooks, that just can't be real either. On a less simplistic tack, a serious consideration of rural life that includes the observation, for example, that life in the woods or in a remote community can sometimes be dangerous or uncomfortable often is met with the same criticism. Maybe there were no chipmunks in the story. Maybe nothing was said about beautiful sunsets or finding meaning in a mountain stream. Still, the very setting is unreal. Contemporary intelligence chooses, for the most part, to deal with the world most of us live in: a world of highways, fast cars, too many people, too little of anything else, stress, anxiety and a value system that has virtually nothing to do with the earth that gave us life. To deal seriously with anything else brings immediate condescension from educated humanity. The mistrust, snickering and disbelief are coupled with something more frightening: an attitude of assumed superiority. To be urban is to be urbane. To love wilderness is to be bewildered.

I suspect that most of us have read about nature in the writings of introspective folks who tend toward hyperbole (once again I feel the incriminating finger of guilt pointing my way). Thoreau never wrote, "I guess you could learn a little from a pond if you stayed there long enough." John Muir never said, "It was an okay kind of mountain." Annie Dillard never penned the sentence, "The gifts of nature are nice, if you like that sort of thing." I also suspect that people who find the writings of people like Thoreau, Muir and Dillard to be naive and simple do so because their own experiences are so pathetically impoverished. They know nothing about the healing, teaching and inspirational qualities of the natural world in general and the remote, undisturbed natural world in particular. Sadly, in the classic gesture of neurotic defense—projection—they believe the stupidity inheres elsewhere.

To love wildness, to choose to live where wildness abounds or at least where it can be found nearby, is thought to be an attempt at escape. A simple question comes immediately to mind: escape from what? If the answer is escape from responsibility, I must disagree strongly. The real responsibilities of human life are not left behind with the city. People still have the responsibility to live and act morally, to question and learn so that issues of morality can be decided on the basis of more than whim or popular trend, to love, to raise children and make both a living and a life. Escape from *society*? Rural man is no less social. In fact, there is reason to believe that when people gather together in smaller communities they tend to be more social. True, there is often the choice to spend time alone in the hills, but all people make the choice to be alone periodically. Is being locked alone in your room somehow more sociable than seeking the solitude of the forest? What is the virtue of seeking solitude by learning to ignore the life that surrounds you as you clatter through dark tunnels riding to work on a subway? Escape from intellectual challenge and stimulation? I have found nothing in urban conversation to indicate that it is, on average, any more intelligent or stimulating than rural conversation. Events differ (few small towns have symphony orchestras, few large ones impromptu discussions at the post office), but the inherent stimulation value of those events differs little. The question remains, escape from what? The answer, often proposed, is escape from the *real world*.

One of the great myths of modern life is this idea of the *real world*. Everywhere you go you find people who believe themselves either to be tragically denied access to the real world (the college student who says, "When I get into the real world...," the soldier who says, "Back in the real world..."), or greatly privileged to inhabit a real world to which others are denied entry (the New York broker who says, "I'm talking about the real world here, not about life somewhere in Kansas!"). The fact is that all of our worlds are real, even if they sometimes appear to be very different. That goes for the rural dweller as well as the urban. It applies to hermit and gregarious socialite alike. Sophistication and urbanity vary from individual to individual, but they have nothing to do with where a person chooses to live. I suppose I'm a bit touchy on the subject. Sometimes after I have spoken with great sincerity and passion about my love for a place, Lime Creek for example, a friend or loved one from somewhere else will say, "Well that's just fine, but why the hell do you have to run away from the *real world*?"

The *real world*. I know quite well the world they speak of. Yes, there are happy times there. There are times when talk turns to matters of weight, when hours pass in conversation from the heart, when untruths and statements meant more to impress than illuminate are left behind. There are quiet moments of understanding and love. There are times in bars and clubs when the fun is hearty and real, when happiness pours from the soul and erupts in honest laughter and song. There is legitimate sacrifice. Legitimate affection. Legitimate joy. There are also moments of pleasure spent in the happy and unexpected observation of the non-human world. There are exotic birds that pass through and coyotes that roam the edges, shiny and dull carp feeding in the rivers, exotic planned gardens and abrupt eruptions of unplanned flora between the cracks and in undeveloped areas. But these are not my dominant associations with the *real world*.

Memories are more than history; they are interpretations. History too is an interpretation, but at least it plays with the illusion of evenhandedness. Memories come, not because we want them and not because we bid them to do so. They come with and within a logic of their own. They come as representations of the meaning of events and not as simple recollections of events themselves. How else to explain what we forget and what we remember? How else to explain the differences in our remembrances at various times, remembrances as different as day and night, as wooded glade and ghetto street, of the same event?

I remember, as a child, listening to the black music of Newark on a static-filled AM radio. I remember listening in my white community with my friend Jerry. I was 10. He was 15. He was a junkie. His great loves were motorcycles (Harleys with millions of reflectors and too much chrome), fast cars and sex. He spoke endlessly about all of them. I remember flying with him and his girlfriend, a woman of 20, at well over a hundred miles an hour along the newly completed Garden State Parkway, scared to death as they laughed hysterically to conceal their fear. Kicks, they called it. I remember the tracks on his arm. I remember that he protected me from the neighborhood bullies. I remember hearing that he was sentenced to life in prison as a habitual criminal. I remember remembering him one day in the woods, after years of not remembering. And I remember that I presumed him dead.

I remember spending Friday nights on Manhattan's Lower East Side, shooting pool in a storefront with Puerto Rican kids who found us quite laughable but came anyway because we had a pool table. I remember them suffering our pompous talk about changing their lives. I remember one of them being whisked off to the hospital in an ambulance as blood gushed between his fingers from the stab wound in his belly. I remember trying to forget.

I remember working in Midtown and walking the streets around Times Square, trying to perfect the art of selective perception, slowly learning not to see the things that were disturbing, not to feel the things that hurt, even though these perceptions and feelings were legitimate and demanded by situations in the *real world*.

I remember living in Newark because I couldn't afford to live anywhere else. I remember taking the train to Manhattan and stepping over the half-dead bodies of winos who slept on the steps of the Erie-Lakawana station at Orange Avenue. I remember getting rolled by two junkies and wondering when I would feel the knife go into my back.

I remember a trip to New York, after I had lived in Colorado for a number of years, to deliver photographs to the 57th Street gallery that was representing me. I remember finding an instructor speaking to an art appreciation class arrayed around one of my photographs. I remember their questions when the gallery owner told them who I was. I remember trying to explain that my photographs were of a world that really does exist in the faraway land of Utah. Yes, those rocks are really shaped that way. No, I didn't fake the sky; it really is that dark.

I also remember being in a bar in the Village that evening with some friends and some people who were not friends, one of whom struck up a conversation about Heidegger. He spoke about his love of Heidegger and poetry and poetic philosophy and a million other things, while I spoke of my love of Heidegger, what Heidegger made me think and feel, and what of Heidegger I could not understand. I spoke from my heart. He spoke loudly, not to me, but through me to the scantily clad woman beyond me who was not supposed to be listening. He spoke from his genitals. Later, I asked a friend why it never seemed that this man was involved in the same conversation that I was. I asked how he could deal so glibly with questions of such meaning and weight. I asked what the hell had happened. It was then I was told that while I thought the man and I were talking, in fact he was performing for the woman beyond. I was not there, and Heidegger had not mattered. In the *real world* my surprise was surprising.

All is not goodness and light in the woods. The mountains do not always fill me with joy. The desert can, on occasion, inspire profound grief. I have been very cold and very hot. Very wet and very dry. I have done some stupid things and nearly died in the mountains, the woods and the desert, but I never remember any of these locations as places of pain or suffering as I almost invariably do the city. I certainly never remember them as places of guile or deceit. Neither, for the most part, do I remember their people that way either.

Huck Finn, with great skill, somehow managed to stay one step ahead of disaster. John Boy's televised fictional life was filled with tragedy and poverty. Still, no one in the *real world* would bat an eye if I were to use either of them as emblems of stupidity and the joyous simple life. What is the source of the urban dweller's condescension and arrogance toward the rural? Perhaps it comes from a sadness imbedded in the wisdom of his genetic heritage, a heritage that cannot be conned by sophistication or fashion, a sadness that the things that really matter are slowly being taken away from him. His sophistication is nothing more than glitter, and his urbanity a flashy veneer. In death the woods will reclaim him, and in eons the glaciers will grind him. I would just as soon return to the forest now while I can enjoy it.

Weaving
the Tapestry

6

Autumn came suddenly to the high country this year. I know that someone says this every year, but this year it actually did. Every year, it seems, on an unusually brisk morning in August, people walk around sniffing the air and remarking, "There's a smell of fall in the wind." The reply usually goes something like, "Yes, I felt it too when I got up this morning," and then continues, "It's gonna be an early winter, I'm afraid." Somehow the coming of winter tempers our love of autumn, and any reference to a change in the summer weather shoots past fall and into the fear of winter. Perhaps that is why signs of autumn are gleaned with something more like intuition than any external sensory perception. We are not so much seeing the arrival of autumn as dreading the coming of winter. After autumn has been *smelled* in the air, it has arrived. No matter that in an ordinary year, even after the mornings have turned colder and the evening nip comes a bit sooner (a normal progression in the waning weeks of summer), the afternoons continue warm and sunny and the leaves continue to flutter in the breeze, flexible and green. Autumn has been sensed and winter is around the corner.

But fall really did arrive abruptly this year. One day it was summer and the next, so it seemed, autumn had come. Leaves began turning and falling off the trees almost simultaneously, and my ultimate test of autumn, the crackling of freshly fallen leaves underfoot, was seemingly passed a day after I had walked the woods in green light and soft wet detritus. Suddenly the light was yellow-orange and the forest floor crunched. Knowing that winter was around the corner I decided to head into the woods for a few days to enjoy the season.

Even though it is somewhat tainted by the realization that the long, deep winter will soon follow, I always greet the coming of autumn with great happiness. There is no time I would rather be in the woods. The light changes dramatically. The angle of the sun is lower, casting longer shadows that bring objects into sharper relief than the flat light of summer. In the deciduous wood, colors become brighter. The air seems fresher and I gain a buoyancy that mirrors the crispness of the air. Carrying a pack seems easier, partly because I am not as apt to become overheated or dehydrated, and partly because of the mysteriously refreshing quality of autumn breezes, which make carrying a pack almost a pleasure.

A pleasure, that is, if you are prudent. I am not. Colin Fletcher wrote in his famous guide for the backpacker, "If you take care of the ounces, the pounds will take care of themselves." I have lived by a corollary: Forget the pounds too; who has a scale anyway? What's the point of going if you don't have what you need? I remember my first overnight trip into the mountains when I carried everything on my back. (Before that, my overnight gear had been carried by canoe or car, and that may be why I still believe after all these years of backpacking that a canoe or a horse is better suited to heavy loads than the human back.)

My first overnight backpacking trip took me into the Sangre de Cristo Range near Westcliffe, Colorado. I was going with two good friends who had recently become backpacking devotees: David and Wanda. David, my backpacking guru, was a prudent and careful person. He was also well read. He knew the ounces beget pounds dictum and he had walked sufficient miles with a pack to know how weight grows late in the day. As I assembled my pack for the trip, I remember the look I got when I tied my heavy tripod onto the top of an already unwieldy load. Answering the silent accusation, I responded, "Hell, David, one of the reasons I'm going is to photograph. I know this thing is heavy, but I need it." I took it. And the first day out I nearly died.

About a mile from the top of Music Pass, altitude, lack of conditioning, inexperience and too much weight got me. We camped before we wanted to on the Wet Mountain Valley side of the pass. Although nobody mentioned it, my load was probably responsible. Morning broke in our short-of-the-goal-camp and was a bit more than we had expected. We had stopped and slept on the border between heaven and earth. The sun rose above a bank of clouds in the valley, brilliant and big in a deep blue sky. Below were the tops of clouds, the sunlit cap of a gloomy fog that blanketed the valley beneath in darkness. The clouds rose and fell, the level undulating below us, never quite reaching us. The steep slope upon which we had camped plunged into the darkness and disappeared. The high peaks broke through into the light, and we sat, bathed in the same light, separated completely from the world below, surrounded by the distorted trees of the Krummholz. It is a scene I will never forget. I had never seen anything like it before, and I have not seen anything quite like it since, even though I have spent many more nights at treeline. Had I not carried too much gear, had I been in better shape, we never would have seen it. We would have moved up over the pass and on into the next valley. Needless to say I photographed the scene, using my tripod, and was quite happy to have lugged it up the trail.

That experience and several others have given me a few rules of my own about the assembling of packs and the setting of goals. First, if you really need it, take it. If you really don't, don't. Learning which is which is a lot like learning other things in life: you make mistakes. But with the passage of time you do learn the difference. As long as a pack's weight is reasonable, a few pounds here or there won't make a whole lot of difference. After a few days under load, the weight becomes a part of your natural burden and life goes on. I no longer consider it prudent to cut the handle off my toothbrush or trim the borders from my maps. It doesn't seem to make much sense to trim a gram of paper from a map when a few seconds later I will be throwing in an extra fly box, five rolls of film and my camp moccasins, just in case. These days I forget about the ounces, load the pounds and let the trip take care of itself.

Still, on this autumn evening as I prepared to head into the Lime Creek area for a few days of photographing and fishing, I eyed my pack with suspicion. I was going alone. Karen was not ready for serious hiking after her ordeal with the transplant. There would be no dividing the weight of community property. I had loaded the kitchen (stove, fuel, matches, pot, pan, utensils, condiments and food), the bedroom (a rather heavy two-man tent made long before the geodesic revolution, sleeping bag and pad), the bathroom (toothbrush with handle, toothpaste, soap, towel, t.p.), extra clothing, survival gear (first-aid kit, compass, knife), fishing tackle (eight-and-a-half-foot rod, reel, line, vest, fly box—just one this time, I had learned something—tippet spools, scissors, forceps, floatant, fly sink, bug dope and the heavyweights: waders and wading boots), and photographic gear (including the same ancient tripod and 120 roll film, twin lens reflex camera that I had carried over Music Pass so many years before). Add in the odds and ends necessary for comfort in the woods and you get a pack that I estimate to have been between 90 and 100 pounds (Karen thought it more like 50 or 55 pounds; we'll never know; we didn't weigh it).

Weaving the Tapestry

There I was with this 100- or 120-pound pack, ready to set off for Lime Creek for some fall hiking, photographing and fishing. Remember how I described Lime Creek as being wild, yet civilized? I held this in mind as I eyed my bulging pack. A road would take me right to the edge of the stream. I would cross the creek, walk as far as was comfortable and make camp. If the pack got too heavy, I'd just park it and set up camp. Forget about the pounds, let the trip take care of itself. And it did.

I drove in and parked where the road runs next to the creek at the valley floor. Shouldering my load, I began to hike upstream through an aspen glade that had partly turned, but remained mostly green. As I walked, the pack became heavier (nothing unexpected here) and I soon decided that there was no need to carry it a long distance. After less than a mile I came to a pool that I had often fished, but not very successfully. If I were to cross the stream here and pitch camp in the glade by the pool, I thought, I might be able to watch it for a while and figure it out. This reasoning, aided by the weight of my pack, led me to do just that.

After my load had been put down and my camp assembled, I worked my way upstream. I fished from about noon until four, working a little over a mile of water, fishing fast and not terribly well. I caught eight fish, missed countless others and startled more than I care to mention from their holds beside and under rocks.

This is often the case when I go to the stream after an absence. There is a rhythm to the woods, to fishing, that is very different from that of work in town. It takes awhile to slow down and find it again. Toward the end of the afternoon, however, the pace of the woods began to take hold of me. I remembered that I was in no hurry to get anywhere. My camp was waiting for me a short hike downstream. I had no clock and no evening appointments. I began to relax.

The last pool I fished had also caused me trouble in the past.

95

Above it, the canyon narrows and becomes a rock-walled gorge. In the pool itself sheer walls contain the flow. Wading upstream is difficult, since the pool is deep and has a swift current. At the head of the pool the gorge makes an abrupt bend of nearly 90 degrees, and the walls of the canyon narrow from the 60-foot width at the tail of the pool to perhaps 20 feet. Fifty feet beyond they widen again and open into steep grass-covered slopes. The foot of the rapid at the head of the pool lies beyond the bend, beyond the narrow walls. It is unreachable by wading and holds the best fish on this stretch of stream. Rarely have I fished it. More rare still are the times I have fished it well.

On this day, after four hours in the water getting the feel of the streambed, finding confidence in my footing and allowing my internal clock to slow down, I decided to try it once again. Usually I would work out as far as possible in the current, and then try to cast a long line up through the narrow gorge and into the wider pool beyond (a tactic that often resulted in bad casts and scattered fish). This time I clung to the narrow walls and worked my way into the mouth of the upper pool by climbing along the walls of the deep gorge. When I reached the neck between the upper and lower pools, I found a ledge from which I could make a comfortable cast of about 40 feet into the water at the head of the upper pool. I was surprised to see fish rising there.

My first cast took a very nice 10-inch rainbow, my second a 12-incher. These I thanked for their meat and killed for dinner. With the trout tucked safely away in my vest, I inched my way back down the wall and made it safely out of the gorge. With dinner secured and a wonderful afternoon behind me, I walked downstream to camp.

Dinner was a celebration of the day. I fried the fish in butter and seasoning and ate them along with spaghetti and bread-sticks beside the pool where I had chosen to set up camp. I watched the currents and the fish that came to feed on the evening hatch of mayflies. We ate together. In the past, with only an afternoon or evening to fish, I had spent little time watching this pool. More often than not I had waded in, cast a line and waded through on my way upstream. I had taken a number of small brook trout here and once, several years ago, a good-sized rainbow from the turbulent water at the head of the pool, but I had never taken a good fish from the deep water in the center, an area I knew had to hold at least one large fish. As I watched this evening I saw a large fish that seemed to hug the wall of rock near the center of the pool. His feeding was leisurely and unhurried. He took insects with a slowness and deliberateness that indicated a sense of security. Few fishermen, I thought, had placed a fly there, or a spinner or worm, and few predators could surprise him there. It was a short trip from the wall to cover in the undercut rock below.

The fish and I enjoyed our respective meals and retired when evening came. Just before sleep came upon me, I remember looking out of my tent and up at the face of Twilight Peak towering above the canyon. It was bathed in the red light of alpenglow, a beautiful sight.

Morning broke with clear skies and unbelievably cold air. My breath was visible, and the walls of my tent were covered with frost. Sometimes mornings like this inspire me to rethink getting up. On lazy mornings I might prepare and consume hot tea and oatmeal from the comfort of my sleeping bag on the ground outside the front door of the tent. After a few more cups of tea, the sun might hit the tent, the temperature would rise and so would I. Unfortunately, on this trip I was camped at the bottom of a deep canyon, so no light would hit the tent until very late, perhaps 10 o'clock. The indirect light of the fall morning was lovely, however cold, and the white trunks of the aspen were glowing in the soft morning light. I had come to photograph as well as to fish, and this light was made for the black-and-white film I was carrying. I prepared and drank my tea from inside my sleeping bag, but was up and out of the tent long before the sun came to warm the air.

The morning I spent photographing along the stream and in the dense groves of aspen that bordered the creek near where I had camped. My mood was quiet and my pace slow. Photographing is something like fishing. If you arrive in the woods with your adrenaline pumping and rush about madly exposing film, little that is good emerges. After time passes and you assume a less frantic pace, images start to come. The previous day and the night in the woods had already slowed me down, and I was seeing a great deal. After a few hours the sun rose above the shoulder of Twilight, and the light, though beautiful, became too harsh for the pictures I had in mind. I sat beside the stream to rest, empty my mind and enjoy the first rays of the sun. As I sat, I heard two sharp cracks, like those of a nearby rifle, and then heard a tremendous crashing. What I saw was a tall, dead aspen tree plunging to earth, its age having weakened it to the point where it could no longer stand against gravity. The earth pulled it down to the forest floor, where it would decay and become soil.

This is a relatively simple event that must happen many times a day in the hundreds of millions of acres of forest on this earth, but it was an extremely startling event to me. I have had limbs come down around me and even seen a few trees fall during storms. Never before, however, had a tree come down near me when there was no breath of wind and no apparent reason for it to choose that moment to fall. The morning, which had begun with magical light, was becoming more magical by the minute. When I rose to walk back to camp, a mule doe that had come close by, probably not seeing me, was startled by my appearance and bounded off into the woods, her hooves hitting the dirt and launching her into flight, four hooves at once, with a sound that I felt in my chest as much as I heard with my ears. Yes, this was indeed a special morning.

Weaving the Tapestry

Later I broke camp, but before wading across the pool with my pack and moving on, I decided to search the water to see if there was any sign of the large fish I had spotted the previous evening. After a few minutes I saw a disturbance that might have simply been the water's flow broken by an irregularity in the rock wall at the edge of the pool, but having seen a good fish there the evening before, the disturbance took on new meaning. Even though I had little evidence to support the conviction, I knew it was a fish. My first cast to the spot was about a foot short, but my second was dead on, and a massive head slowly came out of the water to inhale my fly. When I struck, the fish dove for his home. I was able to force him out into the pool, where he raced about frantically, leaping, tail-walking, trying to escape. Several minutes later, I was supporting with both hands a 14-inch, fat-bellied, brilliantly colored rainbow trout, moving him gently back and forth in the shallow water at the tail of the pool. When released, he went straight for the under-cut ledge of the rock wall. The pool had yielded what was, for Lime Creek, a very large trout, and also one of its secrets.

My hike back to the car through a sunlit autumn aspen wood was slow and filled with thoughts. Any fisherman understands the joy of finally seeing a large fish in a pool where for years he had suspected one, and the added joy of solving the problem of how to land it. Any photographer appreciates the pleasure of a morning spent deep in the woods with glowing light and the white bark of aspen. Any hiker knows the joy of a day, a night and a morning out in the woods, self contained and happy. There had been all of this, and more: a crashing tree, a bounding deer, water ouzels moving upstream with me as I fished, ground squirrels and chipmunks chattering to me from streamside, a splendid wood, a glorious stream, narrow gorges and open riffles. After learning the joy of sharing this place with another and seeing it with her eyes, I was back. This time I was alone, but being alone was not the same anymore.

LIME CREEK ODYSSEY

As the seasons move, we move, going through similar circumstances, but never in quite the same way. There is an old saying that you never set foot in the same river twice. Its flowing water changes. Cycles do not move in empty, meaningless circles—spring to summer, summer to fall, and fall to winter—only to repeat. As the seasons change, time passes and things grow. Some things die. No two autumns are alike. The world is filled with the processes of life, and time is not a simple matter of trajectories. Events are not predictable, and our cycles are not circles, they are spirals. Alone for me now means having been with someone. Alone is different for not always having been alone.

The rest of the day I fished several miles upstream from where I had spent the night. My gear was safely stowed in the car and I knew I would be leaving in the evening, but the unhurried pace stayed with me and I fished well. In a stream that had not changed, in weather that remained the same (the squalls of afternoon snows followed by hot sun), I caught 20 fish, not the eight of the previous day and saw so much more than I had before. It never ceases to amaze me how important it is to spend time in the woods and how much each trip there teaches.

The idea of cycles, of spirals along which we travel, covering the same ground but never in exactly the same way, is certainly not a new one. Although it is manifested in different ways at different times and with different metaphors in various cultures, it is an idea that is universal, timeless and placeless. The idea has become a part of our legends and myths and has been codified in our teachings. Native American cultures speak of the medicine wheel—a symbol, a metaphor and a way of life at the same time. The medicine wheel describes the directions of the four winds and the emotional contents of life. It ties an image to our feeling that we change with the passage of time. This metaphor ties natural reality to our perception of ourselves and our ideas about human temperament. Equally important is the idea associated with the wheel that no position on the path of life, no direction of wind, is inherently good or evil. What matters is change. Change comes with the territory. It is not something we create through an act of will. It is a truth we accept.

Seasons come and go, and we live as they pass, learning the repetitive cycles, keeping our eyes open for surprises. Our moods come and go, and if we are perceptive we learn from them as well. We are alone and we are together with others. We work and we play. We live and we die. In the Judeo-Christian tradition the idea is embodied in the text that begins, "To every thing there is a season, and a time to every purpose under the heaven. . . ." Implicit in the text is this notion of repetitive cycles. Can we be born and not die? When we plant do we not expect to reap? Have we not seen and known the rhythms of life?

Rhythms and cycles are so fundamental to life that it is hard to imagine physical life without them. It is also difficult to imagine the life of the mind without them. John Dewey built his entire understanding of aesthetics on the perception of cycles and rhythms, and I think he hit the mark. What sense is there in a representation, a physical distillation of life in color and image, sound and word, that is not rooted in rhythm?

Our deepest introspection follows similar patterns, and it is in the perception of cycles and patterns, not necessarily in the specific details, that wisdom resides. The history of philosophy is, to a very large extent, the record of man reconsidering the same issues in new ways. The history of individual philosophers seems to recapitulate the history of philosophy. Young philosophy students agonize repeatedly about the same issues, and they move through these issues in abrupt swings between polar opposites. Our thought processes are determined, they fear, by the cultures and values that surround us. There is no genuine thought and no genuine perception; all that we think is structured by our categories, and our categories are given to us by our cultural inheritance.

Alternately, there is the overwhelming fear of isolation, of an aloneness enforced by the inability of separate organisms to communicate. What can we say to each other, not having identical experience, not sharing a common language of words or emotions? The ultimate fear in this case is solipsism: can I know only myself; am I all that exists? Young philosophers also swing between the ultimate epistemological dilemma—fearing there is no way to really *know* anything—and feeling the incredible power of believing they know so much more than anyone else. If there were no spiral in this cycle, the picture would be bleak. Fortunately, with a little time and experience, the issues we agonized over when young become no less meaningful, and their articulation becomes no less important, but the middle ground becomes more clear. This is the ground we travel through as we move between the extremes, the ground that reconciles polar opposites, the very ground that constitutes life. The moving back and forth becomes a moving through in a little different way. Once again we are standing in the river. Although the location is the same, the river has changed.

Remember that old question about angels dancing on the head of a pin? I can remember this question being used to illustrate the narrow preoccupations of medieval scholastic philosophy. I also remember a very defensive medieval scholar arguing that in all of his readings in philosophy and theology, he never once saw this question mentioned. I think he missed the point. At that time in human history we did seem to be preoccupied with some pretty strange questions. Thank goodness for spirals.

There is another familiar old question, one that relates to the nature of perception and existence. "If a tree falls in the forest and no one is there to hear it, does it make a sound?" To a person with any common sense, this question has a simple answer, "Hell yes!" But the question articulates a very real issue. What is sound, the presence of pressure waves in the air or the perception of these waves by a sentient being? Do events exist unperceived? If they do, how does perceiving them make them different from other, unperceived events? This simple question about the tree, through our individual and historical spirals, has raised questions about the meaning of history and of language, about the retelling of events and about the fading of some events into oblivion for lack of human witness.

Then there is the question of non-human witness: if an event is heard, seen and recorded in the mind of a non-human creature, what is the nature of its history, of its existence as image and not present fact? Is language a prerequisite for history? Is this why Heidegger in his gentle anthropocentrism argued that only a human has the power to *world the world*?

Another interesting scientific question asks, if an event is not perceived, can it be inferred from its effect on perceived events? If a tree falls in the forest and no one hears it, will someone see it many years later in the growth of a flower that has risen in the soil that was once its fallen trunk? When must an event be perceived? When it happens? Or can it be perceived, through inference, much later? This last question is precisely the one on which the validity of science hangs. The data of science are presumed to be empirically observed events, but what is the nature of scientific inference? These are all interesting questions, and ones that we may move through many times in life and understand at many different levels. More spirals.

At last our spirals become entwined in something less obviously linear than the development of understanding and less sequential than the fact of growth. At some point our personal spiral becomes a movement we are aware of in a broader context. We see our movement through time and life not as a simple progression and not as the story of a single being (ourselves) or even a single species (man). We become self-aware, and more broadly, aware of a wider world. The tree that fell, the flower that grows in the richness of its decay, our perception of the flower and our inference about the tree, ultimately these all lead us to consider another metaphor: the tapestry of life. The tapestry is neither simple nor static. In many ways it resembles a weaving still in process.

At last Penelope has rejoined us! Staying home, she wove the tapestry of life, the immediate and all-encompassing emblem of the fabric of nature. While Odysseus traveled through his adventures—a simple progression of battles and events, of repetitious victories—Penelope wove. She wove a representation of the complexity of life as a whole, a tapestry that included Odysseus and quite a bit more. She did so while immersed in the fact of place.

When the tall, dead aspen fell in the woods and I was there to hear it, it jolted me out of a state that was more like a pleasant, quiet emptiness than anything else, and I certainly heard it. When the deer bolted because of my presence, it startled me out of my sense of aloneness, although I had never really been alone. Just as mountains and valleys are different aspects of the same whole, so are perceived and unperceived events. So too, nature reconciles joy and sadness, wonderful hope and desperate fear, health and sickness. Life and death. All of these apparent opposites are present in the tapestry we call nature. This lesson I have learned from the rich soil of Lime Creek, from her waters, trees and deer—and from her trout.

The
Naming
of Names

7

High above the forested valleys—above the larger bodies of water that occupy the lowlands—sit the smaller pockets of water that are the glacial lakes of the high country. They can be seen scattered across the land from the summit of any peak in the San Juans, shining in the midday sun like so many gems, brilliant among the brown-gray rock of the crags and the deep emerald of the tundra. They have names, these little lakes, and we read them on our topographical maps. *Lake Como. Parson Lake. Kite Lake. Lost Lake. Trinity Lakes. Verde Lakes. Highland Mary Lakes.* There are stories behind the names. Sometimes there are even names behind the names. Take *Eldorado Lake,* for example. It's there on the map. A name the U.S.G.S. very confidently placed alongside the irregular blue patch that sits beside the tight brown contour lines of White Dome Mountain. The name seems appropriate enough. Many people came to the San Juans seeking riches, and some even found them in the gold- and silver-bearing ores of the area. But Eldorado—as the lake is now known by nearly an entire generation of backpackers who learned the names from government maps, not from the stories that fill the memories and maps of the old-timers—Eldorado once had another name: Annabelle.

LIME CREEK ODYSSEY

Anna Bell was the aunt of a man I know well. Jim Bell is a man whose family is as present in the echoes of the county as the thunderclaps that slowly fade, bouncing between peaks, moving farther away until we can no longer hear them (and not, I sometimes believe, because they have ceased thundering). Jim's grandfather came to this country looking for gold, and he found it. One day, sitting high up in the cold shade of the clouds, he decided to move over to the sunny side of the mountain. There he found an outcropping of quartz that proved to contain one of the largest and certainly the longest-paying lode of ore the county has known. Subsequently, the hollowed-out workings, drifts, scrams and stopes beneath that outcropping became known as the Sunnyside Mine.

If Anna Bell was anything like her nephew (I was not fortunate enough to know her), she was patient, kind, generous and wise. She would have had a wry sense of humor. She would have been a compulsive teacher, as knowledgeable about the history and physical details of this country as anyone, and proud of her place in the history of the San Juans. Jim was all of these things, and that spectacular lake will always be Lake Annabelle for me, because that is the name Jim gave me when he took me there.

He gave me a few other names too. *Grand Turk* is the name the U.S.G.S. gave the pyramid of rock that sits a few bumps down the ridge from the summit of Sultan Mountain. Jim called it *Turk's Head*. So do I. The deep notch in Turk's Head, through which you can sight the peaks of the Weminuche Wilderness from the summit of Sultan Mountain, he called *Gunsight* (some old-timers, in a further deviation from the official line, dare to add an extra syllable to Weminuche, pronouncing it We'-nah-ma-nooch). Gunsight appears nowhere on the official maps. A few miles south of Silverton there is a range of mountains that always catches the last rays of the sun. This range forms the eastern flank of a long stretch of Lime Creek, and from the creek on most any evening you can see the range aglow with the colors of sunset. To the U.S.G.S. this range is the West Needles Mountains. To the locals they will always be the Twilights.

Local names are important, and anyone who believes the origin of names is irrelevant (convention and general acceptance being more important than history) is seriously mistaken. Names, as history, are an important part of our sense of place.

Many years ago a group of us undertook an informal project that we called *The People's Map of San Juan County*. Peaks and places with no names or names we didn't know (or names that were easily modified in the good humor and gusto of a mountain outing among friends) found themselves tagged with handles that connected them to our experiences. A misreading of Gray Copper Gulch yielded Gary Cooper Gulch. A mountain hiked on a day when a friend's husband was in ill spirits became Angry Husband Mountain. The death of a profoundly loved dog, found in the woods with a bullet in his body, inspired the naming of Putney Peak. A whole area was called the Chinese Mountains because it so resembled the photographs and paintings we had seen of the limestone mountains of south-central China. A small rock outcropping above Little Molas Lake is for me, and a good number of my friends, Mount Daniel. Now I have added Karen's Glide and K.B. Rock, places of love and happiness in and along the waters of Lime Creek.

This people's map will never be published. I seriously doubt that anyone has even bothered to write down the names. They live in the minds of a few, bonding us together with our place, with each other and with the experiences that constitute a part of our habitation in this place. Perhaps, in time, some of these names will stick, and our memories, like the memory of Jim's aunt Anna, will become a part of the landscape.

Jim took me to Annabelle during my first summer as a resident of the San Juans. I will never know what it was that made the fates smile upon me so, but it was a rare honor and a trip I will always remember. I will remember it for the country we saw, for the company Jim provided and for the wonderful introduction Jim gave me to the place I would come to know as home. He spoke a nearly continuous monologue as we rolled and bounced upstream beside the Animas River to Howardsville, where we turned and followed Cunningham Creek to Stoney Pass. We climbed Stoney Pass, where we first saw the High Divide, then dropped into the valley of the Rio Grande and parked the Jeep. Along the way he spoke of each mine, each portal, each ruined and rotting cabin, each crumbling mill and tram house. His memory of the glory days of mining in the San Juans was tinged with loss. For him this history was a very personal reality. His life, and those of his mountain ancestors, was intimately connected with mining. It seemed as if each portal, each ruin was somehow connected to his anatomy, as if his body were made up of timbers and ore. None of this surprised me. I had heard a great deal about Jim before we made the trip, and I knew that much of the mining history of the San Juans had been written by his family.

What surprised me was the change that came over him as we crossed the summit of Stoney Pass. Here, dropping into the Rio Grande valley, he spoke less and less of mining, even though we moved closer with every mile to his mining properties around Beartown and Kite Lake. Instead, he spoke in a reverent voice about the streams. He spoke of Bear Creek and Pole Creek, of the trickles that were the headwaters of the mighty Rio Grande. He looked at the mountains that were so evident from our vantage point on the divide. He knew each by name. And each lake. He knew each meadow and glade. Sheep Meadow, Grassy Hill. He named the names. He recalled days and adventures in the places he named, and it wasn't very long before it became quite obvious that this man with whom I traveled through this country was, in fact, a collection of these names, of these places, of these adventures, of the trout he had sought and caught, of the wife he had loved and lived with for so many years and the children he had raised among these hills and meadows, streams and glades. Without this place, apart from these mountains, Jim had no existence. This was his home; this was his place. As important as the mines and mills had been, they were nothing compared to the mountains, even to an old miner like Jim. That, I must admit, took me by surprise.

We shouldered our packs a few miles below the divide, near Beartown on Bear Creek (a few years later I would learn that Jim's nickname among the old-timers was *The Mayor of Bear-town*), and we hiked up over the top. When we got to the divide, we saw the incredible panorama that is the San Juans, a range so complicated and massive that experienced cartographers and geographers throw up their hands in despair when asked to describe it. Somewhere, down in a valley surrounded by those peaks, lay Lime Creek. I did not know it then, but someday it would be for me what the headwaters of the Rio Grande were for Jim. Home.

Jim was full of surprises on that trip. At one point, driving a road he knew well, that I had never before traveled, he turned to me as the Jeep listed perilously to starboard and said with a twinkle, "Don't worry, Steve, she won't roll until she gets to 45 degrees." After a difficult climb over the divide, after we had descended into the bowl that holds Annabelle, after we had pitched our tents and settled in, as twilight gathered around us, he produced two perfectly chilled margaritas in two elegant glasses, their rims coated with salt. While I, a youthful 20-odd year old had been puffing up the trail with my featherweight gear and freeze-dried food, Jim, many years my senior, had been hauling up the real necessities. His eyes twinkled again, and handing me the glass he toasted life, the San Juans, White Dome and Annabelle. Lake Eldorado, indeed. I've a good mind to buy up every map of the county and scratch the name off!

LIME CREEK ODYSSEY

In many ways this has been a book of delicious paradoxes, and Jim personifies them for me. He has a profound love for the San Juans, the crystal clear streams of the high country, the wild trout, each mountain blossom and wild living thing. Great too are his respect and love for the mining that brought man into this place (at least that is what brought European man here in great numbers). There can be no questioning the fact that mining compromises the safety and beauty of the mountains and living things he loves so deeply. Yet his love for each is real and well reasoned. A paradox.

We began this book with the paradox of travel and adventure versus place and quiet learning, of Odysseus and Penelope. It seems to be a part of our shared beliefs that we must travel widely in order to learn, but my sympathies and my respect are with Penelope. I have even presumed to intimate that she learned more in her weaving of place than Odysseus did in all his insane travels and hair-raising adventures.

Then there is the dilemma of our humanity and the difficulty of wanting to be empathetic toward all of creation, of not imposing our human-centered perceptions on the rest of the world when we know it is a nearly inescapable inevitability. This is a most difficult paradox. Where is the resolution? To a large extent, I believe, the resolution comes when we develop a sense of place, when we make a home and become responsible for the long-term consequences of living there. We will never resolve these difficulties if we run away from them.

We cannot come to know a place by rushing in and rushing out. I often wonder just what it is that people see in the wilderness when they come for a week or two each year. I imagine their spirits are refreshed and their time here is quite pleasant. I know they learn a great deal. But what do they *see*? I believe there are some things that can only be seen if you stay awhile. Others become visible only to those who gaze at a landscape and think, *this is my home*.

The Naming of Names

Changes occur very slowly here. There are wagon ruts on the Divide Trail that were etched into the tundra by wooden wheels carrying timbers to the mines. Each year they grow just a little fainter now that hiking shoes and horse hooves are all that are allowed there. The balance and flow of wildlife change with time, eagles leaving and returning, elk and deer populations waxing and waning. Hillsides damaged by grazing slowly recover, while others are destroyed. Burned forests recover, planted forests grow ever so slowly and entire mountainsides are denuded by avalanche. The peaks and valleys of this land parallel the peaks and valleys of our own experience, as these experiences merge with those of others who have made a home here. We know that our time here has an impact on the environment we live in and that we are responsible for the consequences of our actions. Our lives blend into the rhythms of this place we call home.

I am amazed at the uncompromising purity of some visitors to these mountains. Often there is disgust at the presence of a town in a valley as beautiful as Bakers Park. Is their town less ugly because it sits on a plain? Frequently there is disappointment in the presence of mining's rotting remains, but those of us who live here are not solely responsible for this debris.

Once, after falling into a stream high in the mountains (I was scaling a wall above a waterfall), a visitor to these woods stopped to talk to me about what had happened. It was obvious that I was recovering from an accident. My clothes were draped over a branch near the fire. I was shivering in a sleeping bag. The visitor immediately lectured me about the stupidity of wearing jeans in the mountains and the terrible dangers of hypothermia, a subject, I suspect, I knew at least as much about as he. He was wearing a very natty pair of well-tailored wool mountain pants. He was also carrying a magnificent aluminum-framed, heli-arc welded, nylon frame pack, onto which was strapped an ensolite pad and a high-tech geodesic dome tent. I knew that my companions and I were responsible for our own safety and that it meant something that we had managed, in our blatant stupidity, to get me out of the stream, get a fire going and get me into my sleeping bag. To him it meant little. I asked him where he was from. He said California. I mumbled something about too many people, and he launched into a tirade about how mining had damaged the Colorado mountains so terribly that he vastly preferred the mountains of California. Fine, I thought. Go home!

Where the hell did he think his precious equipment came from? Do they grow aluminum on trees? Did he think the wool for his spiffy pants was clipped off the sheep with a pair of wooden shears? Yes, mining has damaged the San Juans, and his needs were a part of the reason. So were mine. At least I had sense enough to know it. Seeing firsthand the tailings piles and the dust clouds they sometimes spawn, the piles of debris littering my home mountains, I know and feel responsible for the consequences of my own wastefulness and greed. I try very hard to control them. I don't think the Californian had any sense of responsibility at all. To him, it was always someone else who was the problem. Seeing ourselves as a part of the natural world, equally responsible for its health and its sickness, is an idea that comes naturally when we sit in a place long enough to see our own impact and know a place well enough to see it change.

I have been in Lime Creek long enough now to have seen a child born while I hiked its woods, to have seen a loved one die while I fished its waters. I have seen a generation pass and another begin to flower. I know the creek will outlast me and my memory. I know there will come a time when all human impact on the creek will be gone. For now, however, we share a place in nature. And I have named that place with my names.

114

EPILOGUE

The winter snow now lies deep upon the waters of Lime Creek, in the forested valley, on the high, windswept slopes above treeline. It began falling toward the end of October. The time when Karen died.

It stopped snowing for several months after the initial storms and began again in earnest in January. Now, beneath many feet of powder, insulated from the bitter cold of nights at high altitude, the trout hold, sluggish in the icy water. Immature caddis flies and mayflies bide their time beneath the rocks and mud of the streambed. Seeds fallen from pods and flowers during the autumn nestle in the decaying warmth of the forest detritus, awaiting their time to blossom. Ptarmigan burrow into the snow, their black beaks and eyes giving them away in the sea of white despite their efforts at concealment, waiting for the rocks and their mottled brown plumage to reappear. Ermine lope through the snow leaving tracks like legged snakes, narrow furrows with paw prints. Spring will come.

Marmots have long since ceased to be active, and along with the bears, have holed up for the winter, somewhat like the people of Silverton. Frost collects inside our windows, and on cold nights inside our doors and walls as well, while woodstoves burn. Spring will come again.

115

Soon the days will be noticeably longer and warmer. The sound of birds chirping will fill the morning with song. One day soon the water of Lime Creek will reappear, the insects will hatch, the trout will feed, the flowers will bloom. The pine marten will argue with me. The eagle will swoop over me. I will stumble and fall again in the icy waters and I will dry again in the warm sun, laughing. Life will go on in Lime Creek—as it always has.